RECLAIM

& UNLEASH

YOUR VIP POWER

VOLUME 2

12 Month Complete Wellness Program to
Increase Your VIP Power to the Max

JENNIFER NICOLE LEE

www.JenniferNicoleLee.com

www.JNLVIP.com

Published by
Live Limitless Publishing Co.
Email: Publishing@sierrarainge.com
www.livelimitless.co

Jennifer Nicole Lee

Contact Information:

Email: thejennifernicolelee@gmail.com
Website: www.JNLCoaching.com

Printed in the United States of America

Cover Design by: Adam I. Wade
Cover Photo by: Joyanne Panton

ISBN: 978-1-952903-07-6

Library of Congress Number: 2020919362

MEDICAL DISCLAIMER

The information is this work is in no way intended as medical advice or as a substitute for medical counseling. This publication contains the opinions and ideas of its author.

It is intended to provide helpful and informative material on the subjects addressed in the publication. It is sold with the understanding that the author and publisher are not engaged in rendering medical, health, psychological, or any other kind of personal professional services in the book. If the reader requires personal medical, health, or other assistance or advice, a competent professional should be consulted.

The author and publisher specifically disclaim all responsibility for any liability or loss, personal, or otherwise, that is incurred as a consequence, directly or indirectly of the use and application of the contents of this book. Before starting a weight loss plan, a new eating program, or beginning or modifying an exercise program, check with your physician to make sure that the changes are right for you.

TABLE OF CONTENT

DEDICATION

VIP POWER DEDICATION

Following the success of our online coaching program at www.JNLVIP.com, and also my 16th book "Reclaim & Unleash Your VIP Power: Highly Effective Ways to Live an Exciting and Fulfilling Life", I felt moved in my heart and spirit, to follow up with a sequel book to help you continue on your VIP journey of success. This book is dedicated to my dear fitness friends and VIP sisters around the world. I am so humbled and honored to spend every day of my life with such royal queens! You all amaze me! The energy you all give me is a big sign letting me know that what I do day-in and day-out really does matter. And that my books, programs, and fitness products really have helped you to not only achieve your fitness goals, but to exceed them. Being a Transformational Life Coach, it is my duty to fill the void left wide open in the wellness industry!

I dedicate this VIP book to every woman in the world who works hard, never gives up, and believes in herself and fellow VIP sisters! This lifestyle program is for ALL

WOMEN, all ages, all shapes, all skin-colors, all sizes, from all over the world! It's a universal program that works! It's for the busy college student, the hard working mom, the 9-5'er, the CEO, and the top office executive.

Now you hold in your hands the blue print for optional VIP success in all areas of your life, and also for achieving that coveted fitness model physique! Your never-ending DM's, emails, text messages, phone calls, and letters of love, light, and encouragement telling me how I helped you achieve your fitness goals are the fuel to my fitness fire. I am successful, because YOU are successful. I know in my mind, body and soul that if I am able to motivate just one person to be better, then I have succeeded in life. To know that I am impacting millions on a global level gives me sheer joy that is priceless. So I thank you, and I dedicate this book to YOU!

I believe that we all share a common goal; to increase the quality of our lives through living a healthy and fit life. Your desire to enjoy a greater sense of well-being has provided me with a continued source of motivation.

May this book awaken the dormant VIP WOMAN in you and strengthen you mentally, physical, and spiritually. May my fitness expertise, insight, and motivation help you to achieve your life's goals and your fitness goals, while bringing health, healing, and happiness into your life. I thank my entire book and publishing team at Live Limitless Publishing who helped me create and design this book as a key to unlock the unlimited potential of my fitness friends. Also, I dedicate this book to my foundation, my three kings: my soul-mate husband, Edward, and our two strong and handsome princes, Jaden and Dylan. I would like to also thank my husband for taking my infamous "Before" photo, which helped me to start my weight loss journey. And thank you, Eddie, for loving me then, loving me now and loving me all through my different shapes, weights, and sizes. You have taught me what real, unconditional love is all about.

And to my VIP clients online at www.JNLVIP.com: I live for training you all online! I love to see you all from every corner of the globe all online working out! From Australia, Holland, Switzerland, to Canada, all over the UK, to even here in the United States-it's just amazing to see how we all are able to connect online and enjoy a solid "kick ass" JNL VIP workout together! We always have so much fun crushing our fitness, beauty and wellness goals together!

And thank you to my best friend, Marli, for believing in me. You are my "life coach", always there to listen to me, support me, and help me find my way. Every day you make my life richer, better, and worth living. You are an angel to me, and I appreciate you! Words cannot express my gratitude for all that you have done to help me and support me!

Remember, keep your VIP power on high, and never bow down to negativity!

In love & light,
Jennifer Nicole Lee

ACKNOWLEDGEMENTS

I want to thank my entire book and publishing team "Live Limitless Author's Academy & Publishing Co." You all went above and beyond!

And to my VIP Queens! Remember, keep your VIP power on high, & never bow down to negativity! This empowering book of strength will help you to always keep your head up high, with your invisible VIP cape flowing off of your back! Let's soar to new heights of success!

Smile,
Jennifer Nicole Lee

FOREWORD

BY YAISSETTE "YAYA" BALARIN

I have been blessed to write this foreword for the book that changed my life, Reclaim and Unleash Your VIP Power Volume 2. That is a meaningful statement and those are powerful words, yet I assure you when you allow Coach Jennifer Nicole Lee and the JNLVIP Power Lifestyle into your life, your senses will come alive, a reawakening begins and you will learn to enjoy living a healthy sustainable lifestyle while creating the life of your dreams. With the multitude of fitness programs, health and diet books, as well as lifestyle coaches emerging daily, Jennifer Nicole Lee has earned her title, Queen of Wellness! JNL shares her daily life with her fans in front of the cameras, on all her social media platforms as well as a multitude of photo shoots for media, print and her many endorsements. JNL lives the VIP lifestyle center stage as she motivates the masses with her beauty, her stunningly fit body, as well as her genuine fun-loving positive contagious spirit. Many have tried to duplicate her success; unfortunately, this industry is full of unproven copycats preying on your vulnerability to get rich with the health and fitness boom but there is only one Jennifer Nicole Lee! Why accept an imitation ghost program or anything less, when you can have live support with the real deal Lifestyle Guru Coach JNL. While sharing her proven methods for success she ensures you get the daily support you need to succeed.

As a successful Author of now 17 lifestyle books JNL has been coaching, educating, inspiring & motivating women for years. JNL's fitness passion, expertise, drive & deep desire to effect positive lasting change is reaching and changing women's lives worldwide. JNL's vision with the JNL VIP Power Lifestyle online fitness and coaching program has earned her the love and respect of a largely diverse group of loyal women followers of all ages. The bond JNL creates with each member she connects with is genuine and proves to be long lasting. JNL Cracked the Code to fitness, health and overall wellness. She then made it accessible in the most inexpensive effective way with the JNL VIP Power online fitness platform. JNL'S vision is a hands-on approach, that is an all-inclusive, fun, refreshing, supportive sisterhood she empowers, uplifts and nurtures daily. She is also a marketing genius creating fun, catchy and VIP Powered exclusive merchandise her fans love. Engaging in this fun, fit and healthy community JNL has created the positive change we need in today's world.

Coach JNL's humble beginnings were tough, she fought on her own most of her life struggling to survive, living day by day. When you are raised with limited resources, no direction and lack of opportunities life may seem dreary, near hopeless. JNL knew she needed to break the chains of the unhealthy multi-generational lifestyle the women in her family lived. Not having the financial means or nutritional education as to what a healthy lifestyle looked like, the options growing up were usually unhealthy, inexpensive survival foods to keep you satiated. When there was a celebration, or a disappointment out came the unhealthy portions of comfort food & treats. When you live with lack and scarcity it is so hard to see the bigger picture. Breaking free from your upbringing, your embedded programmed fears and beliefs sometimes seems impossible or unattainable. The fight or flight instinct is very real and is a defense mechanism used to react quickly for the fight, or as a protective shield, or a means of survival for the escape, the flight. With these dire conditions as your reality you tend to navigate through life aimlessly. Your faith will be tested and may dwindle to almost non-existence as you hold on to dear life. Saving the last ray of hope, the tiny internal flame that has not given up, yet lies dormant in wait is crucial. You see I know first-hand how this feels, this was my life too, this may have been your life & I am here to tell you that it is never too late to turn any situation around. You must believe it!

JNL found a way, she flipped it! Nearly two decades ago JNL gathered the strength and determination to make the necessary changes she needed for herself and her family.

She sought out to create the VIP woman she envisioned by studying nutrition and fitness thoroughly, while training as an athlete. Nothing could deter her so JNL made a bold declaration to keep her driven by entering her first bikini competition. That hard work and determination paid off and JNL won that year's competition and the following year as well. La Tigra emerged as her beauty, confidence and camera instincts were on point and highly sought after. Jennifer Nicole Lee became a world-renowned super fitness model sensation, gracing almost 100 magazine covers to date, spanning nearly two decades! Persistence was the fuel that pushed her forward to reaching her goals by losing 80 lbs then and becoming the super star that has inspired the success in countless lives worldwide. JNL Cracked the Code by living the fit, healthy lifestyle she created. This sustainable program JNL has attributed to her success is the key she created to unlock your untapped potential so other women may follow in her footsteps

Coach JNL has paved the way for all of us and this book is the continuation of her life's mission. Reclaim and Unleash Your VIP Power Volume 2 is a gift from her heart and soul that will set the tone to be the powerful life changing guide you need to create the VIP Power Lifestyle you deserve to live and experience. Coach JNL is dedicated to your success, I know because she believed in me when I had almost lost all hope. She patiently and lovingly listened to me while providing her stellar coaching to educate, as she flipped my mindset as well as my limiting beliefs to Yes You Can. JNL has put forth the motion in my life to create the miracles I now believe are possible. She will do the same for you.

I am a JNL Believer! I belong to the JNL VIP Worldwide Sisterhood!

Join us to be the change you & our world so desperately needs.

Sincerely,
Yaissette "YAYA" Balarin

WHY YOU
NEED THIS VIP POWER BOOK

If you are a long time VIP Queen, or a new VIP queen, you definitely need to read this success guide to living your best and healthiest VIP life. It really doesn't matter how long you have been a VIP. The fact is that you NEED THIS BOOK! Why? Well, for too many reasons for me to start listing off here. However, I will name the top few that are essential for me to cover. Your mind, body, spirit, personal, and professional successes all depend upon YOU! That's right. Not your ex-boyfriend, not your job, not the government, and not the current situations going on in the world. It is up to you to RECLAIM and UNLEASH your VIP power. You are mistaken if you think anyone is going to help you, or that they even care about your success, or what happens to you in the future. It's time to get real! This is why you are reading this message right now. You hold in your hands one of the most potent life-transforming tools that you could ever come across. The time is now. Maybe you've dabbled in self-help. Maybe you started a program and then you shrunk back into your little hermit crab shell to hide away from the world. Maybe you failed too many times and you don't want to fail again. Maybe you got all excited, you were finally going to crush your goals, and 2 weeks into it you were doing so great, until someone hurt your feelings, or something bad happened to you in your life, or something came out of left field unexpected and derailed you. Whatever your past is, it doesn't matter! Why? Because of this VIP fact: The past does not equal the future! Remember, when life gets hard, you must get even harder! You must rip off your rear-view mirror immediately. Why? Because if you are constantly looking back to the past, to direct your future, you are going to keep reliving the past over and over again! And that to me is called insanity! Stop driving yourself crazy and mad by reliving the negative past. Check this VIP Fact: Your past doesn't need you, but your future does! So focus on your future to create the dream VIP life that you deserve!

If you are a current VIP member, then congratulations! You already know firsthand the blessings, miracles, and successes that are yours and you have created by being an active member in our group at www.JNLVIP.com It's essential that you continue! You see, motivation is like a bath. You have to do it daily in order for it to work! So may this book and the new VIP success principles, programs, and practices help you push harder and achieve more in your next level of successes! I also offer coaching one-on-one, to truly dig even deeper into your specific needs and goals! Please visit www.JNLCoaching.com and sign up today if you feel moved in your spirit that you could benefit from one-on-one coaching.

I have some great news for you my VIP queen! This book will give you constant support. There are endless benefits to having constant support. Some of them are improving the ability to cope with stressful situations. Alleviating the effects of emotional distress. Promoting lifelong good mental health. Enhancing self-esteem. Also, you will enjoy physical benefits such as lowering cardiovascular risks such as lowering blood pressure. Research has proved that having a support system has many positive benefits such as higher levels of well-being, better coping skills, and a longer and healthier life. Studies have also shown that support can reduce depression and anxiety. So may this book make you feel as if I'm right there with you, supporting you along the way! If you crave more support, with my one-on-one interactive help to stimulate you on the daily, along with a tribe of women who have like-minded goals, with positive energy, then I highly suggest you join www.JNLVIP.com and also please check out my one on one coaching packages at www.JNLCoaching.com

When life seems to be getting harder, with challenges on a global level, the world can seem very unstable. This is why you must evoke, fuel and nurture your VIP power. This book is so much more than just a book. It is your tool to crush all your goals! No matter how big or small you can and will achieve your VIP dreams and goals! You just have to believe that you can!

And now more than ever, we all need to be reminded daily of everyday miracles. When you have faith, and you stay diligent, and persistent, you can and will achieve your goals. But how can we remain positive when life is getting more and more challenging like never before in history? It's easy! How? You must have strong decision-making muscles. This book will fortify your decision to live a VIP life, infused with joy, laughter, and positive energy, even when challenging situations that are out of your control arise.

The tools, tips and techniques that you will find in the VIP program and this book, will help you crush and conquer all goals, from big to small! Whether it's to find more meaning in your life, to create better relationships, do more of the activities that bring you joy, or if you want to stay accountable, to get clear on your goals, to find a career that you love, to build confidence, or even just overcome the Monday morning blues-YOU CAN DO IT!For the record, I am proud to say that I am a Christian, and I am not here to get into a debate on faith and evolution. However, as your coach, I must remind you of the phrase "Survival of the Fittest". This is a phrase that originated from Darwinian evolutionary theory as a way of describing the mechanism of natural selection. The biological concept of "Fitness" is defined strength and being able to endure hardship. What does that mean to you? That means that life will either make you or break you. Many of us used to let bad things break us emotionally, spiritually, physically, and even financially.

This is where your VIP power will flip the negative situations into positive ones, and you will actually come out stronger! You see once you gain hold of the VIP power principles, and use them in your life, you will take all bad and challenging situations, "flip them" and they will actually make you stronger! That's called winning in life! Not growing weak, but growing stronger from the hard realities of life. Instead of getting bitter, you will get better! Instead of becoming jaded, you will become joyful, instead of becoming sour, you will be sweet! Instead of going broke, you will become financially successful. Instead of failing you will win. Instead of crying victim you will be victorious! Cheers to living the VIP way!

Let's face it, our future is a stake. We must be ready to "push the boulder up the mountain daily". What we used to take for granted, we must protect with all of our might! Life is getting harder as we see, and it's truly a "survival of the fittest" moment! So you must wake up, prime yourself, put on your VIP power, put on your VIP cape, and get your mindset right. In this book you're going to gain indomitable mental strength, actual muscles in your mindset, that will kick in whenever you feel your future is threatened. Our future very well may be at risk. Sadly, a lot of people crack under the pressure, crumble and fall down, thus giving up. However a VIP woman stands tall, gets stronger, and is ready to "push the boulder up the mountain" daily. So let's do this! xo Coach JNL

INTRODUCTION

OPEN LETTER TO THE VIP WOMEN ALL OVER THE WORLD!

For my Current VIPs & Future VIP's in the Making!

Hello, my friends and thank you for taking the time to invest in YOU by purchasing and reading this powerful book! In front of you right now is the master blue print for your VIP success. These words you are about to read will transform your life from "so-so" to "so-so amazing"! If you are sick and tired of being sick and tired you know you are not living up to your true potential, and you know you can do more, be more, shine more, and have more joy & happiness in all areas of your life, then this VIP book and program is for you!

You don't have to stay stuck! You can RISE UP!

Maybe you have let yourself go. You woke up one day, and felt stuck, you felt uninspired, and like you were going nowhere fast. Maybe you are in a fog and you can't see your way out. You feel as if though you've lost your way in life, like you've gotten off track, fell off the wagon, and now are searching and yearning for success in your life. When you look at yourself in the mirror, you don't recognize the once youthful woman full of hope.

You see a tired, exhausted woman who is drained, lost and confused. You look at yourself in the mirror and the reflection looks and feels tired. Deep down inside you desire change, and you wish that you had more energy to get up and go. The job you have may not be fulfilling you. The people at your job are just bringing you down with constant bitterness and negativity, because the reality is, no one wants to clock in at a job that does not fulfil them. You're exhausted from interactions that don't lift you up, and that are draining you.

Maybe every morning when you open your eyes, you just want to go back to sleep because you foresee and expect many problems to come your way in the day. You feel helpless and hopeless. You are afraid of failing again at life, because maybe you have failed before in the past. Maybe you have low self- esteem because you thought you would be further ahead in your life. Maybe it's hard for you to find true joy in your life? Maybe you feel stagnant in your success because between work, challenges, unfulfilling relationships, and obstacles in your life, you have been pushed back into a small little scary corner of being comfortably miserable, and if we're being honest here, you are living a life of mediocrity, Well, this ends today

The once youthful, vibrant person you were is no longer there. She is replaced with a woman who is jaded and without joy. The woman you once were has become bitter and has lost sight on how to be better. You were once so sweet, but the challenges of life have made you sour. Once better, you are feeling bitter. And at one time in your life, you but now you are hopeless.

Well, I got great news for you! Don't worry, because I can and will help you! As a top transformational coach I have created countless success break through's for many people, and now it's your turn

And I am not preaching to you. You see, I once was in these similar situations. I found myself with no drive, no goals and no positive plan of action in my life.

My past is not so pretty. I once weighed over 200 pounds. I had to work 3 dead-end jobs. I had suffered a woman's worst nightmare, a miscarriage, which shattered my world, and I felt alone, scared, and full of fear. I was falling into the trap that my mom fell into, and her mom, and her mom, and so on. You see, my mom was an emotional eater. She ate to console her pain. She over-ate when she really had tough days. She had no schedule, no goals, no plans. I then picked up these habits of self-destruction. Don't get me wrong. I love my mom, and that's the best she could do at the time. However, these unhealthy habits didn't help me at all, and I too began to live my life that way-lost and confused.

My main objective back then, was every day when I woke up, I just wanted to survive and get through another day. I knew that I was heading for the deep end of failure. Once I fell down and out, I knew that I might not get up again in life. I was raised on food stamps by a single mother. I wore hand me downs, and ate free government food. I rode the big yellow bus right up until my Senior high school year. I never did fit in. I was always the underdog, and the odd girl out. I was teased, bullied and always made fun of. It caused me deep pain, and I had low self–esteem. I didn't believe in myself. I didn't stand for anything, so subsequently, I had a tendency to fall for everything.

Then, one day I became a woman on my own. I still ate food to fill my emotional needs. I would do extreme diets, eating little to nothing and obsessively working out. Needless to say, it wasn't healthy. I had no goals and no direction in life. My self-care was non-existent, I was failing to take care of myself. I was failing to love myself properly, and quite frankly it showed.

My personal story gets worse. I had suffered a horrible miscarriage in a 3rd world island with not the best medical care, almost losing my life too. I was visiting Jamaica, with my husband, and we lost our baby. A nightmare that shocked me to truly take care of my health as best as I could! Then I became pregnant with my son Jaden. When Jaden turned one, I got pregnant with Dylan. For a period of 5 years, I was either pregnant, breastfeeding or just down right out of shape with little to no energy. I was at my all- time low! Plus, I had two little precious babies to take care of. So, I knew something had to change, and change fast! I was frustrated, fed-up, and sick and tired of being sick and tired!

My "A-Ha" Moment"

I remember sitting on the couch with my two babies eating pizza and donuts watching TV. I was out of shape, and my energy was zapped. It was as if God spoke to me and said, "You better take drastic action right now, or you will fall into that deep trap of being a nobody, and you won't be able to even take care of your children". It was as if my whole future flashed before my eyes. I was becoming an overweight and unorganized mom who had no direction or goals in life. In that instance, I jumped off the couch, threw away all the junk food, and made my plan of action.

I decided to wake up early, eat clean, workout, exercise, think positive thoughts, set some huge career goals and become the woman that I wanted to be-THE VIP WOMAN! I'm blessed to say that I now run a huge global empire. I am the author of 17 Best-Selling lifestyle books and am a Certified Life-Coach. I am grateful to say that I am living my best life I loving living my life to my fullest potential. I lost over 80 pounds and I kept it off for close to 18 years. I am so fortunate to have loving and fulfilling relationships. I'm so blessed to now be able to enjoy my passion-filled and purpose-driven VIP life!

When I decided that I deserved a VIP lifestyle, I chose to take the necessary action steps required to help me transform my life. And now it's our turn! I am beyond thrilled to share these VIP success secrets in my healthy lifestyle program with motivational workouts, and energy increasing food plans with all of you!

And here is the GREAT NEWS! You CAN transform as well! There is no doubt in my mind whether or not you deserve it. YOU ARE WORTHY OF YOUR BEST LIFE, STARTING RIGHT NOW! It's simple: You must be willing to work for the win that you crave deep within your heart. You can shift the trajectory of your life, you can break bad habits and achieve big goals. And yes, you can become a VIP Queen

Who is a VIP Woman? Who is a VIP Queen

A VIP Woman is a Very Important Person! There are many P's in a VIP Woman's Life that are strongholds of success in her life! They are:

P: Principles-She lives her life guided by the Principles of Success!

P: Plans-She plans her work and then works her plan

P: Programs-She has her own personal program of wellness, success, & joy.

P: Philosophies-She leans on her wisdom and philosophies in life to create the life of her dreams!

P: Productivity-She is productive! She uses her time wisely! She makes miracles and magic happen daily.

P: Pride-She believes in herself, and she loves the beautiful life she has created for herself and loved ones.

P: and a VIP woman is PERSISTENT! She never gives up and always keeps her eye on the PRIZE!

Who is NOT a VIP Woman?

1. A woman who focuses on lack and scarcity.

2. A woman on complains instead of finding solutions.

3. A woman who has a pity party and feels sorry for herself.

4. A woman who believes she is a victim.

5. A woman who doesn't take control and responsibility in her life.

6. A woman who shrinks and doesn't let her light shine.

7. A woman who stirs the pot, causes drama and gossips.

8. A woman who has a low vibrational energy that is always focusing on the negative, not the positive.

9. A woman who is afraid to try and try again.

10. A woman who gives up too easily, and is not willing to fight for a beautiful, balanced and fulfilling life.

Are you ready to do more, be more, and reclaim your VIP Power?

Then take the following Quizzes below:

#1 VIP QUIZ-QUICKLY ANSWER YES OR NO TO THE

FOLLOWING QUESTIONS:

1. Have you gained weight?

2. Do you find yourself often tired or lacking energy?

3. Do you feel stuck?

4. Do you feel like your relationships are draining you?

5. Do you feel like you have settled in your life?

6. When you look into your future, is it bleak?

7. Is your job unfulfilling & draining?

8. Have you lost your purpose in life?

9. Are you frustrated with life, because your needs are being put last?

10. Are you making excuses, sabotaging your very own success?

11. Is the lack of your own self-care negatively affecting other areas of your life?

12. Are you in a relationship with someone who doesn't value you?

13. Do you feel you are being taken advantage of by others?

14. Do you feel like you don't have any voice or say in your life?

15. Do you feel you are out of shape?

16. Do you feel like you have aged, and you get exhausted easily?

17. Do you feel like you always get the short-end of the stick?

18. Do you go to a job that under pays you and under-values you?

19. Are the people in your life users, always taking from you?

20. Do the people in your life put you down, or don't give you the respect that you feel you deserve?

21. Do you look for external praise or validation from others to know your own personal worth?

If you answered YES to any and all of these questions, then this book & VIP Program will save your life!

This is getting good! Let's continue! Take the second part of this quiz to help you gain more clarity.

#2 VIP QUIZ-QUICKLY ANSWER YES OR NO TO THE FOLLOWING QUESTIONS:

1. Would you like to have more clarity in your life?

2. Would you like to live a more fulfilling life?

3. Do you want a job that is fulfilling and fuels your spirit?

4. Do you want to have an exciting future?

5. Are you ready to find your purpose in life?

6. Do you want to enjoy more freedom in your life?

7. Do you want to create healthy boundaries in your life?

8. Do you desire to have more, be more, earn more?

9. Would you like to lose some weight or get in better shape?

10. Would you like to have endless energy, never getting tired?

11. Are you ready to experience an endless flow of success in your life?

12. Do you want meaningful relationships that fulfill you?

13. Are you ready to grow outside of your comfort zone, and to get to the top, where you belong?

14. Are you ready to create the future of your dreams?

15. Do you desire to have more passion in your profession?

16. Are you ready to find your true passion in life and to live it out daily?

17. Are you ready to put your needs at the top of your priority list?

18. Are you ready to stop making excuses and to stop sabotaging your very own success?

19. Are you ready to put your self-care, wellness, and fitness rituals first?

20. Are you ready to end all relationships with those who don't value you?

21. Are you ready to use your voice and let it be heard to demand the respect that you deserve?

22. Do you want to age in reverse?

23. Are you ready to get your dream job that pays you what you are worth?

24. Are you ready to increase the value and quality of your social circles?

25. Do you want to network with people who lift you up & give you the respect that you deserve?

26. Are you ready to finally stop seeking validation from other people, and to validate yourself?

Again, if you answered yes to any of the questions above, then you are ready to become a VIP Woman!

Don't be overwhelmed! You can and will achieve your VIP dreams and goals!

I was just like many women out there who find themselves tired, overweight, broke financially and drained physically until I discovered the success secrets to reclaim and unleash my VIP power! You can discover your personal power too! So, dust off your crown, put it on top of your royal head, and roll out your own red carpet!

Take this 12 Chapter, 12 month, year long journey with me, and let's crack your VIP code together. I'm here to help you transform your life and to reclaim & unleash your VIP Power! Lets do this!

SEASONAL FENG SHUI

IN SYNC WITH THE SEASONS-TO FEEL CONNECTED, GROUNDED AND IN TOUCH WITH MOTHER NATURE & HUMANITY

As you will see throughout this book and VIP program, I will lean into the seasons and special celebrations of the times of the year so we are more in sync with mother nature. Feng Shui teaches us that when you "syncopate with the seasons", you are in sync with the universal forces around you and when that happens, you are more connected to life-force, and more in your groove, you've got your mojo and you are more prepared for anything. This primordial edge gives you more winning VIP Power in all areas of your life!

As a transformational coach, I find that each season has its own natural "activity-predispositions". For example, Spring is a time of spring cleaning, new beginnings and recharging your spirit, so it's the natural time of the year to clean out and start fresh. In contrast, Fall represents the time for harvest, which can represent a to a time for gathering thoughts and researching before moving forward. Winter is a time for family get-togethers, connecting with your loved ones for the holiday season, and hibernating. Throughout we will incorporate our VIP program into the seasons of life.

CHAPTER 1

JANUARY- NEW YEAR, NEW YOU! 4 PART SERIES- PLANTING SEEDS OF YEAR LONG SUCCESS

Happy New Year! Happy new you! January represents a new beginning! But you can't have a new year with an old mind. In this chapter we're going to break down the four weeks of January. We will be covering Mind, Body, Spirit, and abundance which includes financial prosperity and increasing wealth in your life and business.

This month will be dedicated to repositioning you 100% and helping you plant seeds for you to nurture, grow, and harvest throughout the entire year. Throughout this book you're going to be hearing a lot of "farming" metaphors such as planting seeds, watering them, nurturing, growing, weeding out the weeds, and lovingly taking care of your crops. In these chapters, visualize yourself as a farmer looking over your beautiful vast field of abundance, wellness, health, and happiness! On the other hand, when you see people that are suffering, sick, living in that, their field is a baron dry Rock, let no seed would grow in.

Right now take the time to reflect on your current state of your field. Visualize how your garden looks. Is it blooming with beautiful fragrant flowers? Delicious ripe crops? Is it bursting with the harmony of life? Is it beautiful to look at? Is it flourishing with beautiful vibrant colors? Is it a place of rest and positive productivity? Or is it a place of darkness? Contempt? Jealousy? Confusion? And unwanted animals that are preying upon all of your hard work?

No matter where you are right now, we are going to increase your wellness, advance you in your productivity, and rise up our vibration so no unclean thing, toxic energy, or poisonous person can come into your energy field.

Before you begin, I highly suggest you make it a habit to print off your monthly calendar and plan your weeks in advance. Have an intention set for the entire month. January is a vital month for you to press the reset button, to press the refresh button, and reposition you for success.

I like to use an example from one of my past coaching clients. She was living a torturous life, around jealous people, people that just wanted to take advantage of her and not support her. Usually it gets somewhat quiet during the holidays, people tend to "hibernate" during this season. The winter break is a great time for anyone to reposition themselves and use the excuse of being busy due to the holidays, and to shift from continuing old patterns and behaviors. This is the time for you to truly set yourself up for success! When you start the new year, and you see January 1st on the calendar, that is the beginning of the new you that you want to become. If your old friends, or old habits try to drag you back into the past, look yourself straight in the mirror and repeat to yourself "I will not live in New Year with an old mindset." This is where you get to strengthen, and fortify your strongest muscle in your body. YOUR MIND!

Temporary New Year's Resolution vs. a Life-Long Evolution

Before we dive into Week 1 and cover the mind, I want to give you the difference between a temporary New Year's resolution, and a life-long evolution!

VIP Queens don't resolve, instead they evolve! Let the majority of people have their weak, impotent New Year's resolutions! While you create your long life evolution!

Think about it, when someone starts off with their New Year's resolutions, it only lasts for about 2 weeks! Why? Well, many for too many reasons to start listing off here! First of all they have all the intentions in the world, but they have secret underlying counter intentions which cancel out their dreams and goals. It's like having one foot on the pedal of your car pushing the gas, and the other foot on the brake. You're in the same place, stagnant, and stuck! I'm here to release those counter intentions and push on the gas full throttle!

Everyone starts out of the gate really hot. Then real life kicks in and we have so much to do, and we lose our focus on our goals. As your transformational coach, I'm here to give you that daily motivational kick in the butt! I'm here to help you stay focused, and to create a sustainable program that you can do daily without it taking away from your family, work, and to-do's.

Sustainable Program

Many of my past coaching clients have come to me out of frustration. They spent thousands of dollars on high-end coaching and training programs, with a nutritional coach and a trainer. However, the program was so unsustainable and also expensive, that they were only able to do it for about 2 weeks before getting frustrated, fed up, going broke fast and quitting. It was too much for them to handle. They couldn't make it work and fit into their lifestyle. This is where the VIP workout method comes into play. I created this program so you can stick to your goals. You are going to make this New Year's different and this is the year you crack your success code in all areas of your life. Why? Because it is a sustainable program that works for you! Plus its affordable and you won't go broke while getting fit and successful!

The best part? You don't have to work for it! It's simple to implement, it's easy to do, and it seamlessly flows into your already super busy lifestyle.

Why does the VIP Method work? Well, for many reasons! The ability to work out at home is a big success key. By working out in the comfort and convenience of your home, you take out many unnecessary steps. If you went to the gym, you'd have to take the time to put on something cute to go out in public, get your gym bag ready, get your water ready, get in the car, drive, find parking, walk in, have your barcode scanned, and then wander around a sea of cold exercise equipment, sometimes being interrupted by complete strangers that only waste your time. Then after your workout, you'd have to drive home sweaty and wet, come home, unpack your gym bag and then shower. As you can see there are a lot of unnecessary steps that can be taken out if you working towards your goal of just working out. If you take the time to set yourself up for success by creating what we call a "VIP Room", which is an area in your home where you have reserved for your workouts, it solves many problems. Having your VIP room area set aside is also a great solution for time management as well.

And just like you, many of my clients lead very busy lives. So training at home is an effective time-management solution. We just wake up, dress up, work it up, and kick butt! We don't waste time driving to the gym or back. This is really is a great problem solver if you're short on time but long on needing a work out.

DON'T COUNT THE WORKOUTS, INSTEAD MAKE YOUR WORKOUTS COUNT!

From my close to 20 years of experience, I have found that you get a superior workout at home, as opposed to training at a gym. Home workouts are not only highly effective, but allow you to truly focus on you, and not the other people around you in the gym.

How are VIP At-Home Workouts Better than Gym Workouts?

VIP Workouts are better than gym workouts for many reasons. First, when you're at home you use dumbbells and mostly bodyweight exercises. The machines at the gym are big and bulky and do the movement for you. When you're training at home, it takes more physical strength, stamina, and endurance to use dumbbells and free weights. Also your "body becomes the gym", meaning you are not on a conveyor belt called a treadmill doing steady state cardio. But with our VIP workouts you are training 360° degrees on all planes, in all directions. The VIP method truly trains you like an athlete. Not like someone just trying to lose weight. This is why your results stick and it is fun.

Many of my clients have also informed me that since they're training in the privacy of their own home, they are not interrupted by strangers or associates at the gym. No matter how well-meaning these people are, they do take a big chunk out of your time while you are spending it working out in the gym. At home you don't have those distractions. You don't feel the social pressure to make small talk with people you barely know. You can focus on your work out and then go on to your busy day.

I personally like the fact that you don't have to deal with other people's sweat or germs. When you are training in your own home, the only sweat you have to deal with is your own! It's more hygienic and free of other people's germs that you would find in a public place. This is important because as a coach, I've seen people start working out at a gym, they're really off to a strong start, but then they will pick up a virus, cold or flu at the gym their immune system gets knocked out, and they're out of commission for another good week or so. It really puts a strain on their physical fitness level, as nobody likes to get sick when they're trying to get healthy.

On the other hand, in our VIP program, I train you with a focus on boosting your immune system. Always jumping to get your white blood cells moving around your body, with a focus on draining your lymphatic system. As your transformational coach, my goal is to help you have the strongest immune system to fight off any cold, virus, or disease! This is through, of course, movement, exercise, increased circulation, and a healthy Lymphatic system. And of course also food! Food is one of my favorite topics because not only do I love to eat healthy food, there are such healing powers in food. We will cover the importance of nutrition in future chapters as well.

STEADY STATE CARDIO VS VIP WORKOUT METHOD

Ask Coach JNL: Coach, what is better, steady state cardio, or your VIP Workout Method, and why?

When you do steady state cardio, you only burn fat while you're working out. Skyrocketing your metabolism is the bonus of doing the VIP work out method. The VIP workout method is based on high intensity interval training, where you weave in cardio bursts to super spike your heart rate. By using multilimbed compound weight resistance moves that revitalizes and heals your metabolism.

When you recharge your metabolism, you have an increase in EPOC, which stands for "exercise post oxygen consumption". With an increase in exercise post oxygen consumption, you'll be burning fat long after your workout ends. Now that's what I call a good deal.

Why would anyone do steady state cardio? You would only be burning less calories and fat than you would if you're doing high-intensity interval training. You will burn more fat when scramble your metabolism during our VIP workouts by zig-zagging your heart rate up and down numerous times. In addition, I keep your body guessing with new and different workout moves every time we train, so your mind and body never get bored. Plus, you increase your circulation, which is essential in detoxing, and transporting healthy nutrients to every cell of your body.

We practice the undiet diet, or the Non-diet Diet! I call it the "VIP Lean Clean and Green Fun Fit Foodie" approach to eating. Again this is why the VIP method is a sustainable program. One that you can stick to! No more flaking out on your goals, no more not showing up for yourself! This program is so effective, efficient, sustainable, and most importantly, it is fun! And speaking of fun, we're now going to get to our next topic which is getting control of your mind, to make your wellness program so fun, so your mind truly is triggered with so much joy every time you think of your fitness program! That's the VIP way!

WEEK ONE-YOUR MIND

"Your Mind is Your Strongest Muscle
in Your Body. Make it Your Best Friend, Not
Your Worst Enemy. Train it to Always See the
Good in Life & in Every Situation."
-Jennifer Nicole Lee

Your mind is your strongest muscle in your entire body. Not your glutes, not your legs, not your abs. It is your mind! It is what controls the rest of your body, your focus, and what you put your intention on. So, before you start this New Year, you must make an intention about getting control of your mind, and if you don't, it will control you.

They say you can have a mind that is either your worst enemy, or your best friend. And as your transformational coach, I'm here to help you transform any negative self-talk, negative self-image, can lack of confidence into the complete opposite! I want you to daily engage in positive self-talk, positive self-image, and have an embraceable level of confidence!

Sounds easier said than done? Well actually it is very easy! You see, your mind can play tricks on you. All the negative things you think, and you actually play out in your mind, in the future, that haven't happened yet, are all LIES! So if they are lies, you can easily flip them. If you read the first "Reclaim & Unleash Your VIP Power Volume One" book, or you are in my coaching program, you will definitely hear me refer to the notion of "flipping it" many times.

Lets face it!I'm a professional flipper! I've learned the endless benefits countless times of flipping a negative thought into a positive one. For example if you're thinking "I'm lazy and fat" tell yourself instead and "I may not be in the best of shape, but I'm excited about taking positive actions in order to live a healthy lifestyle." Furthermore, if you're thinking "I am not qualified for this position", think instead "I'm hardworking, intelligent, and I pick up quickly on new things, when being trained for a new position." And one of my favorite examples, if you ever think "I am not attractive, sexy, and I don't see why anyone would want to date me" flip it to the opposite to say "I'm sexy, attractive, and you must have really good taste in order to date me"! See how fun it is! Take back control of your mind so you can control your focus! And when you control your focus, you control your outcome!

Set Your Intentions:

I know what you're thinking - "I know this already Coach JNL - I've set my intentions, I've set goals, but I seem to never achieve my goals! I've done so many vision boards, I've written in so many dream journals, but my goals and dreams just stay on the cardboard poster, or in the journal, and never manifest into reality! Help!"

Well I'm going to tell you why!

Counter-Intentions: Let's take a deeper look into the mind. We are hard-wired, shaped and anchored to our collective life experiences to think, feel, and see things the way we do. And this wiring can at times stifle our ability to excel, even when we're doing many things correctly in life.

Have you ever found yourself starting a new year's resolution and then switching to the next thing, and then the next thing, and we don't stick to our resolutions? This is called self-sabotage and can be caused by silent counter-intentions! You can set all the goals in the world, and aim to be highly motivated and still not get the results that you want! So I'm going to show you all the different ways to trigger that growth shift so we can get ready for real results that STICK AND LAST!

How to Remove Counter-Intentions, or to "Get Clear"

There's a middle process in between your intentions being set, and manifesting. I call it clearing or getting clearer. We can say our intentions all we want, but if we have limiting beliefs, or counter intentions, we will move forward and progress. We need to clear these limiting beliefs, or counter intentions asap.

Steps on How to Get Clear, also known as "Clearing"

1. Declare and State Your Intentions/Goals

2. Be grateful! Being grateful that you are NOW READY to finally make life long and lasting results stick. Gratitude is a powerful driving force to getting the results that you want.

3. Now Look at all limiting beliefs around these intentions/goals.

4. Question your false limiting beliefs. They are lies! They are not true. They are not real. They don't exist. Your fear created them.

5. Visualize. Visualize the end result as if it is already happened. See yourself already successful, already healthy, or whatever your goals and intentions are. Really feel within yourself how it feels.

6. Take action! Link pleasure to taking action. Link pain to inactivity. Retrain yourself to fall in love with moving towards your goal, and extremely uncomfortable when you do not take positive inspired action.

Now that Counter-Intentions Have Been Identified, Set Your Intentions, Short Term & Long Term

At the beginning of each year, I like to set my yearly goals. Then, I put my focus on one month at a time. For instance, at the beginning of every month, you need to set your intentions for that month. Then break it down into four weeks. Assign yourself a certain task each week, building upon the next week, so you can achieve your goals. By setting your intentions, you'll be effective, efficient, and get the results that you want. Start with the end goal in mind then reverse-engineer your action plan.

Here you have some action plans that you can do daily in the morning to set yourself up for success every day.

1. Speak your intentions out loud. You know your intentions by heart, but it's so important that you actually verbally share out loud what you desire.

2. Share Your Intentions With Your Coach and Support Group. Did you notice how I said not with your friends, but with your coach and support group? Your friends subconsciously don't want you to do better than them. It's the truth. They don't want you to outshine them, they don't want you to grow away from them, and they don't want you to progress without them. It's human nature. Now if you have a support team, who truly are rooting for you and your rise, that's different. These might not necessarily be friends, but like-minded "soul sisters" that we have in our VIP group. When you share your intentions with your coach and support group, you will now be held accountable. Having accountability is a very powerful driving force behind you making you take action, and continuously working on your goals.

3. Create Success Rituals: Daily Success rituals are imperative to your short-term and long-term success. If you win the morning, you win the day, if you win the day, you win the week, if you win the week you in the month, if you win the month you win the year. If you win the years you win your life! So create a powerful morning routine that you do everyday that will set you up for success for the entire day. Do what works for you. We are all different. Just make sure you have quiet time, you get clear, you write down your

imperative to do list that must be done, and you stick to your daily plan, no matter what happens. Guard your daily success rituals with your life. People will try to rob your focus from them, and pull you away from your goals. Don't let it happen.

VIP FUN WORK-VISION BOARD: Here comes some major fun work! Where you get to dream and choose anything you want in your life to come true for this year! Every January you can work on your vision board which is a powerful tool to help you create visible targets that you will see daily to keep yourself motivated and moving in the right direction! You see, a vision board makes the dream real in your mind, so you begin to believe it's possible! When you make something clearer and concrete in your mind, it feels more real and tangible. You start to believe that you can make all your dreams come true. That's one of the most powerful benefits of a vision board. No it doesn't need to be a poster board that you cut and paste images onto. It could be images organized in an electronic file. Or even a vision journal that you can flip through like a book. The point is to create a vision board, journal, or electrical file that works for you! Anything that'll help you gain clarity and also get you excited about manifesting your dreams and goals. One final tip - make sure you look at your vision board, vision journal, or electronic vision file so you can keep your dreams supercharged and in front of you. Remember out of sight out of mind! So keep your eye on the prize and look at your goals daily.

FUN WORK FOR WEEK ONE: For your fun work for the first week of January I'm going to have you create your vision board, vision journal, or your electronic vision file. Have fun with it! Cut and paste your favorite images that evoke your dream life! Dream big! This is where you get to order anything from the universe! Post on your vision board, journal, or your electronic file the images that evoke joy, excitement, passion, fulfillment, satisfaction, and make your heart burst with so much love! These images should be exciting! If you have a dream house you want to manifest, put your dream house! If you want to attract your soulmate, put a photo of what you would like your soulmate to look like and be like! If you're looking to get healthier and more fit, put a photo of a strong empowered woman that motivates you when you look at her! If you want to crack your nutritional code, and become a fun fit foodie, and eat to win, then put photos of high vibrational meals and recipes on your board! If you want more wealth in your life, put images of prosperity, abundance, and unlimited wealth on your vision board. There is no limit! Dream as big as you want! This is where you get to create your harmonious dream life, that is balanced, and that is fulfilling to you. Make sure you place your vision board or journal somewhere where you can see it every day. Remember what I said, "out of sight out of mind!" Put this positive visual trigger somewhere where you know you will see it daily. It should empower you and not stress you out. Make sure you also put positive affirmations on your vision board such as, "I am strong, I am beautiful, I am successful, I am happy." This is a fun exercise - that's why it's called fun work, and not homework! You should have this done no later than the 5th day into the new year! Realistically you should start even before the new year starts.

FOR CURRENT VIP MEMBERS: If you are a current VIP member in our private group online at www.JNLVIP.com, after you create your vision board, or vision journal, or a digital vision board, – please share it with our VIP group on the Faith-book! There's a power in sharing with other like-minded VIP women who will support you! When you share inside our group, other VIPs quickly rush to cheer you on and root for your goals! This built-in reward system will feel so good that you will want to keep making progress, and stay on your journey!

ACTION STEPS:

If you are not a current VIP member, simply join by going to www.JNLVIP.com and sign up. If you are a current member, please help welcome our new women into our group. Share any and all support that you can! Remember the law of karma - what you give out comes back to you tenfold!

WEEK TWO-YOUR BODY

"Your body is the only place where you have to live. It is the home to your soul. Treat it with love, and it will love you back."
-Jennifer Nicole Lee

In this section I'm going to empower you to fall back in love with working out! If you're already a current VIP member, then I know you love to get your sweat on! But maybe you're a new VIP woman in training, and I need to really transform your thinking from "oh I have to work out, what a drag" to " Yeah! I get to work out! It's so much fun to have a full hour just working on myself!" You see, working out is not a boring chore! It is a fun and exciting privilege! You're giving yourself the best gift ever! To give yourself fresh blood and oxygen to every cell of your body! When you exercise you are going to help your body fight off disease, fight off sickness, age in reverse, and look and feel better!

The benefits of exercise are endless! But many are lost and confused in the world of exercise. I'm here to dispel all myths and to crack your fitness code! You see, for the VIP work out method, I have taken from all different types of work out genres and combined them into one total and complete work out method! You're going to get fat crushing cardio that is good for your heart health and cardiovascular fitness. I weave in strength to help you build sexy lean muscle tone! So you get the best of both worlds in one effective and efficient workout.

Some other benefits of working out is that it is going to help you control your weight, reduce the risk of heart disease, and help your body to manage blood sugar and insulin levels. And it definitely improves your mental health and boosts your mood, and helps you with your thinking, learning, and judgment skills! So the older you get, actually you will be aging in reverse!

"But Coach JNL, I Don't Have A lot of Space to Workout In, Help!"

One thing you might already know from doing my workouts or you will eventually find out, is that the VIP work out method doesn't take up a lot of space to do it in! All you need is a 4 foot by 4 foot space with and a pair of dumbbells to start. And I am just like you! A woman who wants to get in shape and feel great. So I created this workout method for my very own needs and frustrations of not having a lot of space, or a lot of time. I also created this work out method when my sons were very small and were babies and it was hard for me to take them out and about to the gym plus I did not want to leave them in the gym nursery. So, I started working out at home.

There are endless benefits to working out at home. You actually bless your abode with your positive vibes and energy! I love training women in the comfort and safety of their own home! First of all it's very hygienic, as this is where you and you live only! So no germs from anyone else. Second of all that helps with budgeting your time and with time management because you take out all the other extra unnecessary steps that you would have to do if you had a gym membership. We're all busy, and when you work out at home you take out about an hour from your schedule just getting to the gym, and getting back home. And let's face it women, we are extremely pressed for time! We have a lot to do and not enough time to do it in, so if we can save time and our own personal wellness program, this is a definite win!

As your transformational coach, my goals for you are to aim at working out 4 to 6 times a week for 1 hour. If you can't make the entire hour, aim at no less than 45 minutes, as you need to keep your body in fat burning no less than 45 minutes for results to last.

And consistency is key! We can't expect to work out once and then be fit for the rest of our lives! We must plan our workouts in advance.

VIP FIT TIP: In order for us to crack our fitness code, you must use your monthly calendar, or weekly calendar, and go ahead and X out or circle the days you have committed to working out. If it's not on your calendar, you won't do it. Then once you decide on the four to six days you're going to be working out, aim to work out at the same time every day.

Working out in the morning is always best. Why? Because you'll be burning fat the entire day! As a master trainer, this term is called the "afterburn". The afterburn is where your metabolism has been supercharged and it's in a fat burning mode and you will be burning calories all day long after your workout. Many people wake up, go to work, come home, and then they work out at night. For me that doesn't make sense. I rather wake up one more hour earlier, get that workout in and then burn fat all day long, working with my body's natural biorhythms, and then just getting to bed 1 hour earlier. Makes sense, doesn't it? When you train in the morning, it's like you're working out the rest of the day - now that is a huge benefit. So aim to train in the morning so you can enjoy the benefit of burning fat all day long.

Coach JNL, Should I Eat Before I Workout?

As a leader in fat loss, I highly recommend that you workout on an empty stomach. Why? Because you will be burning fat faster, digging deep into your fat stores. In addition, make sure you eat within an hour after you work out because it is the "window of time" where your body needs nutrition the most in order to repair and rebuild sleek and sexy muscle tone. We will get into nutrition later on in our last bonus chapter on the "VIP Fun Fit Foodie Lean Clean and Green" chapter.

PLEASURE AND PAIN: THE CARROT AND THE STICK

Use the principles of pain and pleasure to become consistent and persistent in working out! Link pleasure to working out. Link pain to missing your workouts. Use the carrot to drive you forward, reminding yourself of how great you're going to feel during your workout and after your workout with that after glow, boosted mood and that tight toned body! Use the stick, reminding yourself of the pain of feeling out of shape, lethargic, and lazy, and bloated! You see this is how you get control of your mind! In the first part of this chapter we talked about the mindset, now use your mind to link pleasure to working out and associate pain to missing your workouts!

FUN WORK FOR WEEK TWO: This is where you decide on how you're going to plan your workouts in advance. Are you going to print off a calendar? Put it in your Google calendar? Are you going to put it in a day planner? Do whatever is going to help you stick with it so you always know what day you're going to work out on, and what day is your active recovery days.

I myself am very visual and more "old school". I actually print off calendars that I go in and hand write the days that I'm going to work out on. I put it on a corkboard in front of me, or somewhere where I can see it. This has been a fail-proof method for me. But it may be different for you. You may prefer to create your own calendar, on your iPad, or special calendar software. There is no wrong or right! The fun work that you are to accomplish is finding out the method that works best for you and to stick with it! And honestly the more calendars you have, the better! Remember the VIP principle, "out of sight, out of mind", so flip it and make sure you have your calendars and planners in your sight so they are in your mind!

Use your planning day to commit to the days of the next week you are going to work out. I usually do this on Sunday, my personal weekly planning day. It just makes sense to use Sunday as a good day to plan the rest of the week, and also do your food shopping and meal prep. Look at your family, work, and workout schedule together and like a jigsaw puzzle put into the pieces of your workout in the morning so you're not going to be late to it or miss out on it. You have to look at your workouts as very important business meetings that you cannot miss out on, call in sick to, or not show up to. These business meetings are with the most important person in the world - YOU!

FOR CURRENT VIP MEMBERS: if you are a current VIP member, please share in our online coaching program how you are planning on scheduling and committing to your workouts ahead of time for the week. By sharing, you will be holding yourself accountable, and you will have your fellow VIP sisters and of course your coach rooting you on!

WHY THE VIP WORKOUT METHOD WORKS!

The VIP work out method is extremely potent and powerful because of so many reasons. First of all you will be burning fat long after your workout is over. Your intake of oxygen will increase immensely, therefore making you burn fat longer. This is called "Exercise Post Oxygen Consumption", or EPOC for short. Why? Because I've designed these cutting-edge workouts to stoke your metabolism turning your fat burning furnace into overdrive! How? By supercharging your metabolism with high intensity interval training, infusing heart pumping cardio bursts into multi-functional resistance and weight training movements, mostly incorporating all four limbs, your lower body and your upper body. For instance, Instead of just doing a squat. I will give you a squat with a shoulder raises, so you're working with your lower body and your upper body in the same move. This is going to shock your metabolism and send it into 5th gear! Plus when you're short on time but long on needing some serious visible physical results, this is the way to go.

I have discovered that doing steady state cardio was not necessarily a waste of time, but I did not use my time to its maximum potential. Think about it: would you rather just burn fat while you're working out. Or would you like to burn fat both while you're working out and long after your workout is over? But steady state cardio you're going to only burn fat during the workout. But with high intensity interval training which is characterized by bouts of high and low intensity in different ratios, you are going to have maximum lean muscle mass and optimal fat loss, and even better cardiovascular health! So this is why I endorse and promote the high intensity interval training method and incorporated into the VIP workouts.

My workouts are also extremely effective because we do an assortment of different moves, including burpees, jumping jacks, jump rope, TKO, kettlebell, step aerobics, plyometrics, strength training, plus flexibility and stretching. Doing a multitude of different various moves, will give you a body of a Super athlete!

So if you're a busy mother, work 9-5, a college student, CEO, businesswoman, or just a fierce female that wears a lot of hats and you don't have a lot of time to exercise, but you want max results, the VIP work out method is for you! Plus we change it up so much that you'll never get bored and I will always keep your mind and body guessing.

JOLTS OF JNL DURING THE WORKOUT

Another great feature why the VIP workouts are extremely effective is my motivational coaching called Jolts of JNL during the workouts. I never count, I always coach! I use a 30-second timer and for 30 seconds I have my VIP athletes get as many reps as they can get in during the resistance strength training portion of our workout. We take a little 10-second breather and then go right into our heartrate spiking cardio-bursts for 30 seconds, pushing ourselves to the max. This zigzag training method will wake up a sleepy metabolism. If you feel like your metabolism has "jet lag" and is exhausted or completely broken and shut down, this type of hybrid mix of weights and cardio will revive it! You will be getting fresh blood and oxygen to every cell and truly waking up your entire mind, body and spirit!

THE VIP WORKOUT METHOD IS FOR ALL FITNESS LEVELS

Another great benefits to our VIP workout method is that it's for all fitness levels! It doesn't matter whether you're a beginner, intermediate, or advanced, you can jump right in wherever you are! Since we don't count reps, and I use a 30-second timer for intervals, you're able to lift light, medium, or heavy depending upon your goals or current fitness level. Also, depending on your energy for the day, if you can only get five reps of a bicep curl, then that's great! While on the other hand, another VIP sister might be getting in 15 reps. Again there's no competition! Enjoy the journey and celebrate where you are right now! Don't ever feel intimidated to start! You don't need to be great to start, but you need to start in order to become great.

FOCUS ON LUNG CAPACITY

As a master trainer, I always have my athletes focus on increasing their lung capacity. I always have my clients inhale raising their arms over their head and then exhale bringing their arms down. What does this do? It actually opens up the lungs to be longer allowing more air to flow in. My intentions and goals as your trainer is to have you build the healthiest and strongest lungs ever! Why? This allows you to get more oxygen into your body. When you have more oxygen in your blood, you will have an increased EPOC. EPOC stands for exercise post oxygen consumption. When your exercise your post oxygen consumption is increased, you will burn more fat and also have more energy. It's like having five workouts in one. And that's exactly why my clients are not only getting results, they are having their results stick!

Here is a very effective VIP breathing exercise method that I created. I call it the 3-6-9 breathing technique.

- Inhale for a count of 3.

- Pause at the top of your breath and hold.

- Slowly exhale for a count of 6.

- Repeat this 9 times.

Afterwards you will feel refreshed, rejuvenated, with your lungs expanded. When you're inhaling, visualize you're actually filling up a balloon with air, and you want to blow out the bottom of your lungs! Expanding your lungs to full capacity will help you increase your athletic performance as well.

Now here comes "Professor JNL", Class is in Session"

As a top transformational coach with close to 20 years of experience, I learned that there are a lot of F's that equal an A in fitness! Use this fun take on "making F's" to fuel your fitness fire for the entire year and beyond!

8 F's That Equal an A in Our VIP Program

Here are my top 8 F's that equal an A and will put you on the fast track to success!

1. Focus: I teach my clients worldwide to tap into the power of focus! Aim to focus on getting ready for your workout, to even having a strong focus while training during your exercise program. When you are working out, nothing else exists except for the move that you're doing! Block all distractions that are competing for your attention. That's one of the major self-sabotaging things that people do is that they allow their focus to weaken, and take their focus off of their goals. So tap into the power of focus, and make your fitness program and wellness rituals as your top priority.

2. Full range of motion. When I see many of my clients working out, they will do a half rep thinking it's a full one. However, you must do full range of motion from the bottom of the move, to the top of the move. No cheating, and no cutting corners.

3. Fight: you have to fight for your right to be fit! Sometimes life will give us a low blow, knocking us to our feet. But that's when you need to get back up and fight for your right to be fit. Fight for keeping your workouts on your schedule no matter what. I can't tell you how many times I've heard from other women that they had dealt with

devastating situations, a crisis, or a personal setback-which pretty much wiped out their entire fitness program. Fast forward a year later, and an entire year went by and they did not take care of themselves and they let themselves and their health go to the wayside. You've got to fight for your right to be fit. No matter what, I am at getting 4-6 workouts a week and, and I will eat lean, clean, and green!

4. Fearless: you must be fearless when you're going into your VIP workouts, and fearless when you're planning your weekly schedule. Be fearless when you wake up all the way until the time you go to bed. Know that life isn't easy, but when you're fearless, you will match any obstacle or challenge toe to toe, head on! And you will be victorious!

5. Friends: Friends are so important! Make sure you associate yourself with other like-minded fitness friends, who will root you on, support you, and really cheer you on to your fitness success!

6. Frequency: You must be frequent with your workouts. You don't work out once, and then you are fit for the rest of your life! It doesn't work that way. Just like a bath – you don't take one bath, and then expect to be clean your entire life. So you have to be consistent with your workouts. Train for four to six times a week. So plan your workouts in advance, as if they were important

business meetings you cannot miss, call in sick too, or just flake out on or not show up to!

7. Fun: it's so important to make your fitness program fun! Why make it boring and dreadful! Some of my fitness clients have coined me as the Queen of livestream workouts, and when I go live through JNLVIP.com, I always make it a point to not only exercise my clients but entertain them! It makes all the difference when I see them laughing while they're doing burpee's! They don't even know how hard they're training, and they're actually rewiring the brain to associate pleasure, happiness, and joy to the experience!

8. Faith: last but not least, you have to have Faith! Why is fate so important to working out and your wellness program? Because it is the foundation that everything rests upon. You have to have faith in your abilities, you have to have faith in yourself knowing that you will train up to six times per week, you have to have faith in yourself that you will not sabotage all of your hard work by eating unhealthy. So when you exercise your faith muscles, you are already setting yourself up for success, not failure!

As we end this section on faith, let's jump to Week 3, your spirit in the next section.

But first let's close out on your fitness & food goals for January:

Aim to workout 4-6 times per week. Keep your eating lean clean and green!

NOTES:

_____

_____

_____

_____

_____

WEEK THREE-YOUR SPIRIT

I think this might be one of my most favorite sections of our entire book! Why? It's because the spirit must also be fed daily with motivation, love, light, support, and community. That is the VIP way You are not alone in your fitness and wellness battle! You see, people overeat because they are spiritually suffering inside! I call them "the hungry ghosts" of pain, despair, worry, doubt, anxiety, past hurts and pains.

Let's face it. As adults we have been hurt so many times spiritually. We've had our spirits crushed. We've had our spirits stepped on. We've been taken advantage of. We've been used. We have been abused. And we have been overworked and underappreciated. That can riddle one's spirit with a lot of pain and suffering. But it's up to ourselves to heal ourselves. It's not anyone else's responsibility but ourselves to take 100% percent ownership of our pain and then turn it around, flip it, and heal ourselves of our own pain and suffering. When we harbor pain, resentment, guilt, shame, blame, and all those negative emotions, we make our spirit sick. And when you live with a sick spirit, you cannot, I repeat, you cannot have a healthy mind and body or heart.

So in this week dedicated to healing the spirit, and creating a lifestyle that supports living a healthy, vibrant, fun-loving, joyous, and exuberant spirit that is always bursting with happiness, we will talk about living a purposeful life, that creates balance between physical psychological, and social aspects of human life.

My goal as your supercoach, trainer, and more importantly friend, is to help you to grow and nurture a loving solid relationship with your higher power. No matter what you call your higher power whether it's light, God, your heavenly father, the source, your creator, the universe, it is important for you to start daily giving praise to your higher power, and praise your creator the entire day, and end your day in also praise and gratitude. Why is this? Because when you know that your higher power is watching out for you, and the universe is working for you and not against you, there's a shift in perspective and your paradigm that is extremely powerful and positive for you.

It is so refreshing to see more and more people recognizing their own spiritual wellness. I love to see that there is a growing recognition of the importance of spiritual health as the foundation for physical health and overall well-being. Positive beliefs comfort your spirit. And the strength you gain from a healthy spiritual relationship with your higher power through prayer, meditation, and positive spiritual reading, can contribute to your spiritual health.

My goals for you this week are to improve and strengthen your spiritual health by exploring your spiritual core. Ask yourself the questions of who you are, what is your life's purpose, and what do you value most. Always look for deeper meanings in life and analyze occurring patterns that will help you to see that you do have control over your destiny. And that by being positive, you actually bring destiny helpers into your life. Being aware of this can help you achieve a happier and healthier life.

Also having a community of other like-minded women like we do in our online VIP coaching program, allowing you to express what is on your mind will help you maintain a focused healthy mind. So communicate, share, and connect! We also enjoy deep detox stretching sessions which can help improve your spiritual wellness by reducing emotional and physical strains on the mind and body. My sessions help to lower stress, boost your immune system, lower blood pressure, and also reduce anxiety, depression, fatigue, and even insomnia. I always stress the importance of thinking positively.

Nothing positive can come out of a negative mindset. Once you start doing things in your life in a positive manner, you will find yourself totally seeing things differently and having a stronger focus on your mind, to control it to be happy and healthy.

VIP FIT TIP: Aim to always take time during the week to meditate. I highly suggest you pick a certain day of the week and at the same time to help you manage your stress, and connect with your inner self. You have to do the inner work in order to enjoy the outer work. Also this is one of your many VIP Powers!

You must know when you are on a brink of a breakdown, so you can stop, meditate, realign yourself and instead have a breakthrough! By meditating, you'll be able to purge the negativity out of your life. If you don't let go of toxic energy in your life, this could very well be a detriment to your spiritual wellness. You could actually get "spiritually sick", bringing your vibration down.

Flip your stress into relaxation by meditating. This will help you to have a stronger relationship with your higher power and increase your spiritual wellness.

FUN-WORK FOR WEEK THREE

Know that God, your higher power loves you and supports you. Think about it, every thought is an actual prayer. Thoughts are words that you don't speak. So if your thoughts and beliefs are turning negative, flip them into positive! Instead of throwing a pity party, throw your praises up so the blessings come down. Another part of your fun work is to get rid of toxic people who bring your vibration down. These toxic people are dangerous. You must get them out of your life because they are going to become a detriment to your spiritual wellness and make you spiritually sick. Remember as you strengthen your relationship with your higher power you will be increasing the intestinal fortitude and the spiritual muscles to take out all toxic people from your life.

NOTES:

_____

_____

_____

_____

_____

_____

_____

WEEK FOUR: ABUNDANCE

Okay - many of you have been waiting for this chapter! You are like "Coach JNL, show me the money! I want more of the green stuff! I want to have millions of dollars in my bank account!" Well before we go demanding the universe of all the millions that we want, we must release all counter intentions that are secretly blocking our success.

Sadly enough, many of us were raised in an environment where money and being wealthy was secretly looked upon in a negative light. We silently were being programmed straight into poverty. It's even on the news and through some popular media outlets that the rich or the wealthy are evil people, and they worship money, and they put the value of money over the livelihood of other people's well-being.

Well I am here to clarify all of this. In my VIP coaching program, I am here to make spiritual millionaires out of you. Well if not millionaires, wildly financially successful angels that have one foot in the spiritual world and one foot in the material world. Look at Oprah Winfrey for example. She runs a very spirit focused empire, always giving back to tons of charities.

She has founded several charities underneath the umbrella of her companies, and continues to give. However she is one of the wealthiest women at the same time. My goal is to help you obtain that same balance where you look at money and being financially free as 100% healthy for you, crushing all counter intentions and subconscious mental blocks that are secretly blocking your wealth from entering into your lives.

First of all, abundance comes in many forms. We must crush the notion that being wealthy only comes in the form of money. Abundance and prosperity comes in multiple forms in this limitless and never ending and ever-expanding universe. Here is a VIP principle that never fails! Increase your value in your life, you will increase your wealth. When you invest in yourself, learn a new trade, get a new core certificate, and constantly add to your resume, I know first and foremost that this is a direct form of abundance. Adding value to yourself will create more financial success. So continue to do the inner work so you may manifest the outer work.

If you want to see more money in your bank account every time you check it, make sure you always live in abundance. What does this mean? Never say the words "I wish I could afford it". Never say "I can't afford that". And don't ever have these words coming out of your mouth "That is too expensive for me." Right then and there you've already told the universe that you are not worthy of living a financially free life full of prosperity and abundance.

If you've been a current VIP member for some time, you know very well just how much emphasis I put on the power of words. What you talk about you bring about. What you say, you will manifest. So flip it!

Instead of saying "I wish I could afford it", say instead "I am worthy of it, and I'm receiving it now."

Instead of saying "I can't afford that", say instead "I can't afford that and even more."

Instead of saying "That is too expensive for me.", say " I have great taste! And I'm so grateful that I can afford what I want."

<u>VIP POWER PRINCIPLE:</u> Did you feel that shift? Where your intention & attention goes, your energy flows. When you flip the negative phrases into positive you instantaneously transform your intention, attention, and your energy! You transformed your energy from one of lack and scarcity into prosperity in abundance. Your brain automatically started creating ways for you to create the wealth that you deserve. The secret is to keep at it, be consistent, and keep reshaping your focus and therefore reshaping your abundant future.

Top VIP Ways to Attract Abundance Into Your Life

Gratitude: If you're a VIP - you will see that the law of gratitude is a powerful moving force that transforms any moment from a negative one to a positive one. You can use the law of gratitude also to increase more abundance in your life. I always say how can you expect to receive more, if you're not already grateful for what you already have! Repeat after me " I am grateful for what I already have, and I am receiving more." When you stop and look at everything you have, the roof over your head, your personal belongings, and everything that is yours, it is impossible not to feel grateful. When you're grateful it becomes a powerful magnet that attracts more blessings of prosperity and abundance into your life. So practice the VIP principle of gratitude. Wake up with an attitude of gratitude, and don't let anyone kill your VIP Vibe of gratitude!

See It, Dream It, Visualize It: Use the VIP Power of visualization. When you visualize yourself with a dream bank account, earning the type of money that you know you deserve inside, and living a beautiful life of comfort that is sustainable, you put a psychic Demand on the universe and start moving all the pieces to fall into the right place. and it's true, everything begins in the heart and the mind. Every successful wealthy person began their success in their mind. They dared to Dream Big Dreams! And they believed it was possible. So take some time to allow yourself to visualize. I visualized a lie. So make it a part of your daily rituals to visualize you living your dream life. Dre in the possibilities for yourself, your family, and your loved ones. Sadly enough a lot of us allow our dreams to grow old and cold. Well I'm here as your VIP coach to reignite those dreams! I'm here to Fan the flames as the only thing that comes out of visualizing and dreaming are results! Plus it's free!

Shift Your Mindset: You must let go of all black and scarcity thinking. For the past 17 years in the industry transforming people's lives, I saw that wealthy people live in a world of abundance. While poor people live in a world of limitations. Those that are poor in spirit will be poor in Pocket. Poor people think there's not enough to go around in the world. That is a fear-based mindset. Their answers are either or the other. But never both! In a poor person's mindset they go for security above all, safety before self-expression, and protection over possibility. On the other hand, wealthy people understand that I'm being productive, and using their creative talents, Plus a willingness to be bold, Brave, and have courage, with an open mind, they can have both! Or as I say 'I want it all"! and there's nothing wrong with wanting it all – because you deserve it all! You must build your life on the "Both" mentality, you will see the opportunities that you are once blind too.

Create Your Wealthy Empowered Reality:

We are co-creators of our own reality right now. Every thought, every word, and every action creates the next second of reality in your life. You have so much power in your mind body and spirit, that you don't even know! Sadly enough we are not being very intentional about the reality we want to create. Let's have fun with this one! Write a list of things that empower you and motivate you to move forward in your life. Create this inspirational list of thoughts, things, activities, and other people that pushed you, and Empower you to be full of wealth and happiness! Write down on your list the exact things that make you feel more confident, bold, courageous, and brave, and that give you the audacity to move forward on your success plan. And let's contrast this with another list, on the other side I want you to list the things that demotivate you or demean you and move you away from your goals. Let's be real, society forces us to live more in the realm of this low-vibrational list. It kills our motivation. As your coach, I'm here to flip that. No more living at 10%, 25%, not even 50% of your potential! Wwe are going to ignite your financial freedom, Empower you to attract the abundance you deserve, and supercharge your energy so you raw to you the exact Prosperity that is right here right now with your name on it.

Positive Affirmations that Attract Abundance: One powerful way to rewire your mindset to attract and also create the unlimited and Limitless well that can be yours is to daily repeat some of these empowering wealth inducing affirmations below.

> I can and will have more than I ever dreamed possible
>
> I feel good about money and deserve it in my life
>
> Great wealth is flowing to me now.

I now create my wonderful ideal life.

I am thankful for the comfort and joy that money provides to me.

I know I am abundant.

I always have enough money for myself.

Everyday in every way, I am becoming more and more prosperous.

I see myself as wealthy and that's who I am.

I choose wealth and abundance.

My wealth arises from honesty in everything I do.

I am worthy of great success

I love abundance in all its beautiful forms

I am wide awake to my abundance

I release all my negative beliefs about money and invite wealth into my life

I am prosperous healthy, happy and live in abundance

Making money is good for me and for everyone in my life

My income is growing higher and higher now

Money is an important part of my life and is never away from me

All my issues with Wells have disappeared

I clearly see opportunities to every last lie make money

I am wealthy

Whatever I do it always ends in amassing wealth

My greatest good is coming to me now

Out with the Old, & In With the New! Detox & Cleanse:

As you find tune your abundance vibration, now is the perfect time to declutter, detox, and cleanse your surroundings. Take everything that no longer serves you and you can liquidate it into some fast cash by enjoying a garage sale, or putting it up on eBay, or selling it on LetGo, OfferUp or Etsy. There is a metaphysical and magical transformation that happens when you get rid of objects in your home that are clogging your flow of wealth and abundance your way. If you feel that your wealth attractor Factor has been stagnated, it's maybe because you are holding on to things that are no more value to be of you and you simply don't have enough room to allow the new abundance into your life. So this new year new you, make the time to get out with the old and in with the new.

True story, I had one of my VIP members take my advice when January, she got everything that no longer served her. She had a garage sale, also listed things on eBay, and also used the luxury reselling platform called "The Real Real" to sell her designer handbags, fine leather goods, such as shoes and belts. At the end of all of her sales, she tallied up over $5,000! Talk about liquidating things that no longer serve you, creating the wealth in the Buns that you need to empower your new wealthy, happy, and healthy lifestyle!

So use her story to empower you and look all around you! You were sitting on hundreds if not thousands of dollars of unamused stuck wealth. Transform it now into money that moves and you can use to invest into your successful dream future life!

In Closing:

Abundance is everywhere. It's our job to open our eyes and to see it! When we acknowledge just what a huge immense Universe we live in, abundance will start flowing your way. Practice all of the above fun-work exercises and start seeing prosperity, abundance and financial freedom flowing your way!

NOTES FOR CHAPTER 1:

_____

_____

_____

_____

_____

_____

CHAPTER 2

FEBRUARY- THE MONTH OF SELF-LOVE AND SELF-RESPECT-PLANTING SEEDS OF LOVE

How can you expect others to love you when you don't even love yourself? So I am here to help you turn up the love! February Here We Come!

Happy month of Love! In February the entire world celebrates the holiday of Love, Saint Valentine's Day! This is one of my most favorite times of the year will we celebrate not only love between our soulmates and significant others, but we must turn that love back to ourselves and soak it all up!

Self-love, self-respect, & self-care are the three guiding principles for this month! We're going to enjoy fun self-care rituals such as dry brushing, foam rolling, and yes even marrying ourselves! This is going to be a month like no other! Why? Because we're celebrating the most powerful emotion which is love! And sadly enough we give love to everybody, even showing love to complete strangers! But when it comes to showing love for ourselves - that's where we make the biggest mistake. We withhold from ourselves the very thing we need most, which is love!

The reason why many of us do not practice self-love, self-respect, and self-care is that quite frankly society makes us feel guilty for actually taking care of ourselves. It has been tainted with people labeling these essential activities as conceited, vain, excessively proud of oneself. stuck-up, self-absorbed, big headed, narcissistic, self-congratulatory, snooty, and high-and-mighty. No wonder people get stuck in a rut! Just when they start having results, and gaining confidence, and traction in crushing our goals, they get negative backlash from everyone else that might be slightly jealous! Or we may get negative energy from those that don't have their own goals and self-love, respect, or care VIP program in order. In this chapter, I'm going to help you break the chains that have been holding you back from being the best version of yourself! I'm going to help you take off the noose that has been on your neck that was very slowly closing in on your very right to live a vibrant, colorful, joyous, and healthy lifestyle to the max! I'm going to support you and make sure that you practice self-love, self-care, and self-respect rituals!

WHAT IS SELF LOVE?

Self-love, in our "VIP World", boils down to not creating hell for yourself. Why? Because others will create hell for you! All kidding aside, self-love is essential to your well-being. Some describe self-love as having a regard for your own happiness and living a life to increase a better sense of well-being. This is not a moral flaw! This is not vanity or selfishness! This is actually the opposite. When you take care of yourself from the inside out, you're giving everyone around you a better more loving and understanding version of yourself to live with. It truly is a gift to yourself and others. It's not conceded to eat lean clean and green. It is not selfish to work out four to six times a week. It is not egotistic to practice at home wellness rituals such as meditation, prayer, journal, or enjoying a hot bath or a cup of tea. Whatever floats your boat and makes you a happier VIP - DO IT!

Some fun examples of self-love are making sure you get your workouts done, and eating optimally for maximum health benefits. Also enjoy at-home spa rituals such as an epsom salt bath, a rejuvenating meditation, a facial, foot massage, or even a power nap while listening to a guided meditation. So make sure you schedule in some wonderful down time! I personally like to enjoy a hot relaxing bath with my favorite aromatherapy oils, and also listening to some relaxing music to wind down my energy. It's very soothing and I feel so luxurious! And best of all, you can do it in the comfort of your own home!

How do you plan on practicing self-love: Write below:

_____

_____

_____

_____

_____

_____

_____

_____

_____

_____

_____

_____

_____

_____

_____

_____

WHAT IS SELF-RESPECT

When you look up in the dictionary the word "self-respect", this is what comes up: pride and confidence in oneself; a feeling that one is behaving with honor and dignity. Having self-respect helps others to see and treat you with dignity and worth. Often the backbone of self-respect is knowing your values and living by them.

Having self-respect often means that you need to stand by your character and be willing to defend your values and actions. So if you are a longtime VIP, or a beginner, we are going to implement daily self-respect rituals such as our workouts, positive thinking, goal setting, and making sure we eat antioxidant-rich highly nutritious meals made with our favorite superfoods.

EVERYONE IS ON YOUR TIME! Don't have to answer emails or texts the moment you receive them. Reply when you are ready to!

YOU PUT HAPPINESS BEFORE MONEY: You have to have money to pay your rent, mortgage, and your bills. But you also have to find satisfying work that fills your spirit. Remember to always put your happiness before money.

NEVER APOLOGIZE FOR WHO YOU ARE: Remember VIP Queen! You must hold your head up high because you have a crown on top. If You bow down to others who do not respect you for being yourself, your crown will slip and fall off! Don't ever start a communication with the words I'm sorry or please forgive me. There's nothing to be sorry for, unless you made a mistake.

YOUR WORTH IS NOT IN HOW MANY LIKES YOU HAVE: Your life is not about how many followers you have on Instagram or Facebook! You find value in your true VIP sisters, your real friends, and supportive family members.

SOMETIMES YOU LOSE TO WIN: a VIP woman picks her battles. She knows that there are many moments when it's absolutely essential to speak up and stand up for her VIP power. And then there are other times when that energy is simply not worth it. I'll be up he knows when she needs to "lose" to "win".

DO YOU FOR YOU: be 100% you! In our VIP group, we never judge each other. Whether you decide to wear your hair long or short, dress up or dress down, or you decided to have or not have children, or you're vegan or a meat eater, your lifestyle choices are yours alone. As your coach, I know that together they make up who you are!

SELF-ACCEPTANCE: let's face it VIPs! We've all grown into a different person with different goals and values then who we were in our twenties. We can't stay up late like we used to, or even drink alcohol the way we used to! And that's okay! And your life may be different than what you envisioned it, but we are cool with that and have a great sense of inner peace. Its all about self-acceptance.

LOVE THE SKIN YOU ARE IN: I started my weight-loss journey when I was over 200 lb. But the last time I started my transformation, I started from a place of love, not hating myself. So I'm here to tell you that you must love yourself. Love your body as it is now! Whether you have 10 pounds lose or a hundred pounds to lose you need to start your wellness journey with self-love and always practice self-respect with positive self-talk and by having a positive body image.

BE AT PEACE WITH KNOWING THAT NOT EVERY ONE WILL LIKE YOU: Celebrate who you are. And be at peace with the fact that not everyone is going to love you or gravitate towards you. You're going to waste your energy trying to change their mind. Think about it this way, you can be the ripest, juiciest peach in the world, and there's still going to be somebody who hates peaches. That's just the way life is. And remember acceptance is the greatest healer.

KNOW THE POWER OF THE WORD "NO": It's okay to say no. It doesn't mean you're being mean or rude. you are free to say no to any social invitation when you feel like you rest. You can walk away from any situation that makes you feel uncomfortable. And when you say no, say it firmly!

Now this is the exciting part where you get to evaluate how you plan on practicing self-respect!

When you implement self-respect into your daily habits, your life just flows!

Write below your favorite self-respect rituals that you really identify with:

_____

_____

_____

_____

_____

_____

_____

_____

_____

_____

_____

_____

<u>FUN WORK FOR FEBRUARY:</u> You can't cheat on a marriage and expect it to work. The same thing goes with how you treat yourself. So our fun work for this month of love is that we're actually going to marry ourselves! Yes, you heard me right! This is one of the most powerful exercises and rituals that you can do! And every year you will actually renew your vows to yourself!

Write Your "Wedding Vows" To Yourself!

We are going to use this time and space below to actually write our wedding vows to ourselves. These are commitments that you promised yourself to do. We as a team are going to hold you accountable!

Here are my own wedding vows to use as a guide or inspiration for you to write yours in the blank space!

I , Jennifer Nicole Lee, promise myself to practice self-love and self-respect in all areas of my life. I will not allow anybody or anything to disrespect or dishonor you.

I promise to make sure you get your workouts on time, aiming at 4 to 6 workouts per week. I make the commitment to eat lean, clean, and green in order to get optimal nutrition full of super foods that are high in antioxidants.

I promise to make sure that you get undisturbed, adequate rest so you will be refreshed and recharged, and rejuvenated on a daily level.

I promise to always flip negative thoughts or emotions in order for you to feel your best.

I promise to always remind you of all the things, and blessings you have to be grateful for so you will remain in an attitude of gratitude.

I will make sure that you stay focused on your well-being, mind body and spirit!

I will work very hard to help you vibrate higher, and keep negative energy vampires away!

I trust and honor you, now and forever!

Now have fun and write your own wedding vows below:

_____

_____

_____

_____

_____

_____

_____

_____

NOTES FOR CHAPTER 2:

CHAPTER 3

MARCH- MARCHING UPWARDS & ONWARDS, NEVER LOOK BACK

Spring Has Spring! Spring Ahead

Look forward to your bright future! Never look back, only just to check to see how far you come! Let's rip the rear view mirror off, as we cannot create our dream life by constantly looking into the past! Our past does not equal our future!-JNL

This month we celebrate you taking the time in January to map out your entire year's goals. And then I applaud you for following through by executing certain action steps covering your mind, body, and spirit. We then took the time in February to focus on our self-love, self-respect, and self-care. Now this is where it could get tricky. Many of us want to shrink back to our old ways and outdated habits that no longer serve us. As we might experience feelings and situations that are uncomfortable. Well I'm here to tell you to get comfortable with being uncomfortable! This is the jolted lifestyle! If you're comfortable, that means you're not setting big enough goals and you're not living in your purpose! You see, we must go through some essential growing pains that help us get us to where we want to be in life. So this month, I'm going to make sure that you keep marching upwards and onwards and never look back or shrink back to your old habits. We must push through to the other side! We must continue and be consistent and persistent with our action steps and keep our eye on the prize.

What To Do When We Get Negative Reactions from Others:

VIPs! So you are on the right path. You are making huge strides in your VIP wellness program. But sadly enough when others see that you finally got your "shift" together, not everyone is happy for you. Even close family members and friends are giving you the side eye, making negative remarks and even going as far to make shady comments.

What do you do? These negative responses almost force you to shrink back into your hermit crab shell. I know I've been there! During my several attempts before I cracked my fat loss code for good, I was on such a strong path and then a curveball would be thrown my way with negativity from my so-called friends, toxic associations, and also even complete strangers.

- "Why are you eating like a rabbit?"

- "Why are you starving yourself?"

- "Why are you working out so much?"

- "Who are you trying to look hot for?"

- "How did you lose the weight?"

- "Did you do weight loss surgery?"

- "Aren't you hungry all the time?"

When you are asked these questions, you can feel uncomfortable. It makes you want to hide, and even go back to your old habits. But I'm here to push you even further! In this section I'm going to share with you some VIP hacks to help you out smart sabotagers. Whether they are harmless and they don't know they're being annoying, or if they're out to truly ruffle your feathers, either way, you are going to be set up for success and know how to handle these unwanted questions and also the unwanted attention.

And it's true as the old adage goes "It only takes one bad apple to spoil the bunch."

If you are willing and able to get rid of that one bad apple", then I'm here for you! On my wellness journey I had to be throwing out bad apples right left and center. Along your path of success, you're going to come across those who are out to sabotage you and kill your VIP vibe.

We've all experienced the effects of this firsthand of negativity, even more so when we are really trying to create a healthy lifestyle for ourselves.

You must be wary of negative people, as emotions can actually be contagious.

Emotional contagion is real and does exist! It describes the fact that moods transfer between people over a short period of time. And yes, many studies have proven it!

So my point? Get away from negative people. You cannot win with them. Many sadly enough are narcissists and manipulators. They don't want to see you doing better than them. So when you have so much at stake, and you're on a positive path, please get rid of all the bad apples.

On the other hand, this can be wonderful when you surround yourself with happy people. This is exactly why I created the www.JNLVIP.com group! Many studies have shown that when you surround yourself with like-minded people, who are also supportive of your goals and on the same similar paths of wellness, you will succeed and never go back to your old negative habits.

I call people energy vampires who suck the life right out of you and who are extremely negative.

Stay away from energy vampires. People who constantly express negativity, or are asking 20 questions, and are not supportive to your new wellness program are like emotional black holes. Everyone who comes in contact with them suffers the consequences. I'm actually looking for fang marks in my neck after they leave because it's like they suck the life right out of me. Then on the contrary there are your VIP sisters who are super supportive for you! They jolt you! They help you turn up and on your VIP power! This helps you soar to new heights and success!

QUESTION: "But Coach JNL, How do I deal with these Energy Vampires and guard my VIP power and stay on my path?" Easy! I got your answers right here!

In order to minimize the impact of negativity in your life, consider two scenarios:

1. Mentally take your "Immunity Shot" to their negativity. And avoid "infection" when others bring negativity to you. Don't pass it on!

2. And stopping your own personal negativity when you feel it creeping in and lowering "good mood" neurotransmitters, such as your dopamine, serotonin and oxytocin! Because you don't want to spread negativity to others when you find yourself in a negative mood.

Be mindful of your own thoughts and actions, You will be able to navigate these scenarios like a pro!

Below are six strategies I've implemented with success in my own life as well as countless success stories from my VIP Queen clients. Read over and start implementing today.

Dealing With Negativity & Jealousy in Others

When you are celebrating your VIP power, unfortunately you're going to end up dealing with negative and jealous people. And yes you're also on the daily going to find angry, grumpy, and frustrated people wherever you go. It could be co-workers, your mom, or a complete stranger.

No matter how these folks treat you, remember that A VIP WOMAN IS ALWAYS IN CONTROL OF HOW SHE REACTS!

If your goal is to continue on your VIP wellness program, lose weight, gain energy, and tone your sexy lean muscles, then keep reading! Below are my top hacks to help you navigate through the channels of negativity!

1. Flush It! Lose to Win! And Don't Take It Personally

Many people are like garbage trucks. They drive around full of crap, garbage, full of frustration, full of disappointment, and full of anger! As their garbage piles up, they look for a place to dump it. And if you let them, they'll dump it on you! So don't let them! But if someone wants to dump on you, don't take it personally. Just smile, wave, wish them well, and move on. Believe me. You'll be happier. And then FLUSH their GARBAGE down the cosmic commode.

You see, I did not say start a debate, and fight! I call this "lose to win". Many narcissists and manipulators like to spark a fight to get your feathers ruffled. But if you stay calm, cool, and collected you will be able to actually win this battle. By just smiling, waving, and wishing them all well, and moving on, you actually won the fight. You saved your time and energy and dodged that bullet.

And it's true, we never know what someone else is going through in life.

Give others the benefit of the doubt by "assuming the worst". Maybe their boyfriend broke up with them, or they found their husband cheating on them, or their pet is sick, or a family member is dying of a chronic illness. Let's give them the benefit of the doubt. And yes, their negative actions probably have nothing to do with you. They're just expressing a negativity and you happen to be there to receive it. But if it's a family member, co-worker, or someone you have to live one, please skip to Chapter 11 for November on how to create healthy boundaries that will protect your well-being.

2. The VIP 10 Second Negativity Rule

When life turns negative, you don't need to turn negative back. If someone says something nasty to you, or throws a shady comment, is downright rude, don't react. Instead be proactive and follow the VIP 10-second negativity rule. Counting from 10 to 1 backwards, take a deep breath and slowly count 10, 9, 8 and so forth until you get to one. As you're counting down think about why they're acting this way. And think about how you can evoke a positive outcome without looking like a pushover. Many people are looking to provoke thoughtless reactions out of us. But a VIP woman does not give into impatient urges. Instead we take a deep breath, create that mental space to act with intention.

For example, when responding to a jaded family member, or a fake friend who is out to throw you under the bus, or negative coworker, take some time to digest by counting from 10 to 1 backwards. Set yourself up for success by always taking the high road. A VIP woman never reacts back abruptly. She always takes a power pause, and assesses her best positive way to respond back.

How to March Upwards and Onwards:

As your transformational coach, I'm here to push you over that uncomfortable threshold that divides your old, archaic, outdated you, and the new you that you are now working on that is currently under construction! When you're at the crossroads between your old self and your new self, you daily have to make decisions. We can approach our new VIP selves with confidence and dedication, or we can shrink back into our old selves through confusion and fear. You are not a turtle, that when life gets hard, you stick your neck back in your shell to hide! Remember you are a VIP Queen and you hold your help up high!

This phenomenon is called "Approach-Avoidance". You associate pleasure with approaching your goals, but then when external negative responses occur, you then switch sides to associating negativity and you flip from approaching your goals, to avoid in your goals.

This is where you must mentally get tough! You must link so much pleasure to continuing on your goals. This is a little bit of a hairy and uncomfortable time of your transition. I call it a transition crisis. But these stormy waves will soon calm down if you just keep pushing to the new better you. The old people that are triggering you to shrink back into your old self will eventually get sick and tired of bothering you, or actually fall to the wayside and disappear out of your life. In return as you continue to grow in your new VIP womanhood, life will bring you the angels that you deserve!

Destiny Killers vs Destiny Helpers

Let's have some fun! Think about your VIP Wellness Journey as a story that your writing. There's going to be your fairy godmother, your tried and true sidekick partners, your best friends until the end characters, and also those ride or dies. And on the flip side you're going to have the villains that are out to kill your destiny. So in your story called life, you need to look for the helpers, the destiny helpers as I like to describe them, also known as angels. One of my most famous sayings is when you believe in angels they appear. So look for them! Look for the genuine sweet spirits that are authentically there to help you and push you to the next level of success. Steer clear of the destiny killers. You know the ones that make you feel bad for absolutely doing nothing. The ones that make you feel guilty or ashamed just for being you. It is completely up to you to get rid of all destiny killers within your control and power. It'll make your VIP wings spread longer allowing you to fly to your ultimate level of success just that much easier! Stay away from the destiny killers who are out to clip your wings or put you in a cage. Remember you were born to fly!

Why the Past Doesn't Equal the Future:

The time has come. The time is now. The past does not equal the future. If you have failed in the past in any area of your life, you must flush it. We are sometimes too busy looking through the rearview mirror at all of our past failures and we're bringing that energy into the future. Rip off the rear-view mirror and throw it away! We must march onwards and upwards, never looking back! If you have to leave some toxic people, negative habits, or judgmental family members in the past, please do so! You are now at a crossroads. Remember if you continue to act in the same way, you're going to get the same results. If you are truly watching to replace all the negative energy in your life with positive, again stop looking to the past and bringing it into the future. You must look 10 years ahead in advance and see what type of life you want to live. And then reverse engineer backwards.

Remember this VIP Success Key: If you want to succeed in your life, remember that the past does not equal the future. Just because you failed yesterday, one second ago, last week, or 10 years ago, THAT MEANS NOTHING! All that matters is RIGHT HERE, RIGHT NOW!

Success is a numbers game! Keep your eye on the prize!

BURN THE BRIDGES, BURN THE BOAT

If you are in a situation and you burn your boats or bridges, you destroy all possible ways of going back to that situation. So donate away all the big clothes that you no longer want to wear or fit you and are too baggy for you. Get rid of your monthly subscription to the gourmet cake company. Stop hanging out with that toxic friend who loves to go drinking at happy hour and munch on endless bowls of chips and salsa while she slams down pictures of margaritas. Stop taking your negative family members phone call which only send you into a downward spiral of emotional eating. Stop texting back your ex which is nickeling and diming your energy one text at a time, pull the plug on the monthly wine subscription from Napa Valley Vineyard that only fills you up on empty toxic calories triggering you to order fried appetizers from Uber Eats. I am so jolted, can you tell?

It's time to burn the bridges and burn the boat! There is no retreat to your old self. Not on my clock! How many times are you going to do the dosey doe? Or I call it the Texas two-step? You're going to take two steps forward, then two steps back, you're in the same darn place where you started. You're like a gerbil on a wheel going nowhere fast! It's time to burn the bridges and never look back!

WHY COMMUNITY & SUPPORT FROM OTHER LIKE-MINDED WOMEN ARE ESSENTIAL TO YOUR LONG TERM SUCCESS

You can't do it alone! It's as simple as that. The journey will be hard, difficult, and very lonely. When you have a chance at getting healthier, losing weight, and getting in shape alone, it seems just that much more difficult! But when you have support from other like-minded women, and an online community full of other fellow "VIP sisters" who are rooting you on, your wellness journey is so much more fun!

Psychological research has found that a group approach helps, as it's easier to stick with a **weight loss** plan when you have **support**. It's true that we find some sort of comfort, security, and calmness about our wellness program when we see other women on the same VIP path as us. We can identify. We can relate. We don't feel so isolated. And this is where the magic and miracles happen! This is where our beliefs transform into knowing!

It's so cool to see the lifelong relationships that we cultivate just from checking into the VIP "faith-book" group. The priceless camaraderie that enforces our daily habits is crucial to our collective long-term success!

Emotional support counts, too. Groups that gather to share day-to-day weight loss victories and challenges can be an enormous source of encouragement. It makes you part of a community, which can be a big deal.

Remember when you tried to do it by yourself? All those restricted diets made us feel so lonely. It was hell on earth! But now, with a VIP group of Queens just one click away, there's no reason to feel alone!

VIP Support

Let's get real, life is hard. And just because we have decided to get healthy, sometimes we think it's all going to be unicorn and rainbows. However it can be the exact opposite. You're going to have good days and bad days. But when you're a VIP, pretty much all your days are good! However, if you're feeling stressed out and like you might slip up on reaching your goals, log on and talk through it with a fellow VIP sister who's in the program. And yes, you are allowed to vent in our VIP group! Because you can't deny how therapeutic venting is!

Look, I am also here as your "Coach-on-Call" and I know you will regain some of your determination to stick with your VIP weight-loss plan.

It's Not Bragging if You Can Back It Up!

Lost a Pound? Brag about it! Went down a smaller bikini size? Brag about it! You finally zipped up that zipper on your favorite pair of skinny jeans? Brag about it! Make sure you also let people know when you've reached a milestone in your program, like when you've lost 10 pounds! You see, it's ironic that when you are crushing your goals, and slaying your accomplishments, not everybody's going to be happy for you. The minute you tell someone that you lost five pounds, they're going to make a snarky remark such as "It's probably just water weight you gain it back in a day, don't get too excited!"

However that's not the case with our VIP group! As your team leader, I cultivated a community and online culture where we cheer, and cyber root for each other when goals are met. It is such a healthy feeling to root on your fellow VIP queens who are accomplishing all of their dreams and goals. And yes, you too will feel good about sharing your achievements! Let's be honest: sharing your accomplishments can be a good thing! And here is the magic "VIP Sauces" the positive feedback will encourage you to continue your efforts.

Being a part of a community also has the potential to increase your chances of losing weight. According to a study published in the Journal interface, participants who showed the highest amounts of social embeddedness saw the biggest results by losing more weight than those not in a group! Now that's the power of group effort for you!

March On! Have the Confidence to Keep Moving Forward

So you're continuing on your VIP program. Your friends are getting jealous. Your so-called soulmate is making rude remarks like you were conceited or too self-absorbed you're always working out. What do you do? You keep moving on! It's like fine tuning an instrument. You keep on tuning and tuning it until it's perfect. Either these people will get with your plan, or they will weed themselves out. But most importantly you must move on to become the best version of yourself. So march on! Have faith and confidence to keep moving forward! Don't look back! Don't second-guess yourself! Don't doubt yourself! Have the resiliency and the intestinal fortitude to be the best strongest version of yourself! Don't worry you will find your real friends on your Wellness VIP Journey! Upwards and onwards

Spring Has Sprung!

Spring Has Sprung! Spring Cleaning! Time to Spruce Up! Shift from Winter to Spring

Happy Spring. Happy New Beginnings. Happy You.

Spring has sprung! I love this time of year. What a miraculous season! The beautiful thoughts of spring flowers, Easter bunnies, little yellow chick-a-dees just makes us all so happy! Spring is extremely symbolic, with themes of rebirth and renewal. Spring also refers to love, hope, youth and growth. The seasonal symbolism for this period may also allude to religious celebrations such as Passover or Easter, a time of spiritual rebirth! It's also a time for Spring cleaning, usually reserved for the third week of March when we put away all of our winter blankets, winter sweaters, and clothing as the weather turns warmer and we pull out our spring decorations with flowers, Easter baskets, with beautiful playful colors and pastels.

Coming out of the cold winter, many of us are eager to feel spring, thus calling this urge "Spring Fever". To help usher in this new cycle, I suggest you dive right into spring cleaning, mind body and spirit and of course your blessed abodes.

There are many VIP activities that you can do to help usher in and celebrate this new time of the year. Queens, enjoy implementing these VIP seasonal rituals, so that you can feel an improvement in yourself, your space and your VIP program.

Home is Where the Heart Is! Clear and Clean Your Living Spaces

How do you have less stress? Get Spring Cleaning! Yes, it's true. When you organize your personal space, you get to enjoy a more well-kept and organized environment, which in turn relieves stress. Stress levels can also be reduced just by cleaning. Personally, I find cleaning to be very therapeutic! So get to dusting, folding and organizing! In addition, this physical activity counts as cardio too! It's a win-win.

The saying "out with the old and in with the new" is commonly associated with the new year. However, it also rings true for Spring! We instinctively love to Spring clean! First of all when the weather gets warmer, it simply makes sense to put away all the winter clothing and blankets, allowing you to tidy and spruce up as you do so.

It's a spiritual law of metaphysics, when you clear out your junk drawers, garage, basement, your closets, and even your refrigerator and wallets, you're making room for fresh new energy to come in.

Think about it, after you clean, tidy up, and organize your personal living space, don't you feel a great level of satisfaction afterwards?

Go one step further! Cleanse the energy of your space with some sage.

Benefits of Saging or Smudging

Sage purifies the air in your home. The most-used types of sage have antimicrobial properties. This means they keep infectious bacteria, viruses, and fungi at bay.

Though scientifically unproven, burning sage is_thought to release negative ions. This is said to help neutralize positive ions.

Some common positive ions are allergens like:

- pet dander

- pollution

- dust

- mold

If this is the case, burning sage may be a blessing for those with asthma, allergies, bronchitis, and other respiratory conditions.

Not only are we going to clean our homes, we are going to clean and clear those cobwebs from our minds, bodies and spirits.

Spiritual Windex: Let's throw out the mental clutter! It's time to get rid of the mental clutter, which are the negative thoughts, fear based thinking and self-doubts. Maybe some unfavorable things happened over the holiday season, which you are still mulling over. Or past negative experiences keep coming back up into the forefront of your life. Let's break out our "spiritual windex" and nip this negative energy in the bud.

Flip It: When these negative memories start to make their way into your brain, first acknowledge them for a moment as if you are stepping outside yourself and observing your own thought process. With your awareness focused on those particular adverse and damaging thoughts, visualize that you are now releasing them – that they no longer fit in your brain, they no longer serve you for this new VIP time of your life. Then replace them with something more empowering and positive right away. I call this "flipping it". You catch it and then you flip it. In addition, prayer and meditation are ways to help strengthen your inner strength and resolve, giving you clarity in times of chaos.

Don't forget to also schedule in some quiet time. A little planned alone time can help you identify any head garbage cluttering your mind and heart. Try deep breathing, meditation, journaling or spending time in nature to tap into your spirit.

<u>Cleanse and Detox Our Bodies:</u> Its detox time! Time to recharge our bodies and hit that "reset" button. This is the perfect season to start a fun detoxing program.

I suggest you do a green juice cleanse or a fat-fruit-flush-detox and cleanse.

Break out your juicer and dust off your high-speed blender. Stock up on fresh fruits and vegetables. Don't forget the ginger and turmeric as these are beneficial also for cleansing the body and reducing inflammation.

When you do a detox and cleanse, besides focusing on the obvious benefits of purging your body of toxins, be mindful of the concept of cleansing and renewing all areas of your life. The inner cleanse can also coincide to your outer cleanse, as you can enjoy ridding yourself of any of your undesirable attributes while decluttering your environment. When you declutter all areas of your life together, this will lead to a more effective and lasting transformation!

Spring Season Produce: Say goodbye to "Old Man Winter" and hello to fresh, vibrant Spring produce. Eating fresh foods is the perfect way to rejuvenate your body this spring. Take a trip to your local farmer's market and stock up on in-season favorites like asparagus, tomatoes, spinach and strawberries. At the same time, clear out your kitchen of any high calorie comfort foods, or high-sugar, high-salt and fat-laden processed foods that you may have stockpiled during the winter season.

See Your Doctors: Now is the time to schedule your annual wellness visits, if you have not already done so. A big part of true long lasting wellness is taking care of your overall health, and this means scheduling any routine blood tests or regular, annual checkups. I highly suggest of course your mammograms, and also pap-smears. If you are over the age of 45, also book your colonoscopies. If you are age 50 to 75 years old, you should get screened for colorectal cancer. The U.S. Preventive Services Task Force recommends screening beginning at age 50. Some groups recommend starting earlier, at age 45. The vast majority of new cases of colorectal cancer (about 90%) occur in people who are 50 or older. In order to be safe and not sorry, I suggest you start as early as you can. I'll never forgot when one of my good friends got diagnosed with colon cancer in her 30's. Please don't let this happen to you. Early screening doesn't hurt. It can only help.

Reenergize your VIP Exercise Routine. The best way to stick with your VIP program is to make sure you schedule them first in your new Spring calendar. Many say "carve out the time to work out". I don't agree with this notion. Instead of trying to fit it into your spring schedule, make it the top priority of your day. You see, since you train in the comfort and convenience of your own home, you have less wasted time. Get your 4-6 VIP workouts in per week! Since the weather is also warming up, you can enjoy some time with G.O.D. , which is short for "Great Out Doors"! Enjoy a nice walk, or burn calories outside in the garden by digging and planting.

Spring Ahead-Look Ahead

In a true VIP fashion, how are you set yourself up for success in the spring will flow right over into the summer! So make sure you do a strong spring cleaning for your Mind Body Spirit and your physical space. Enjoy decluttering your mind as you declutter your surroundings. The stronger your spring cleaning, the stronger your summer season. And when we spring ahead, we never look back!

FUN WORK FOR MARCH

As we close out this chapter for March, remember to look for the warning signs when you want to shrink back into the old version of yourself, picking up the negative habits that did not help you. When you see them, reassess the situation. Ask yourself "if I go back to my old habits, where will I end up?" and "Who and what is causing me to shrink back to the old me"? "And "And what can I do to continue on my VIP Wellness Journey for me?

_____

_____

_____

_____

_____

_____

_____

_____

_____

_____

_____

NOTES FOR CHAPTER 3:

_____

_____

_____

_____

_____

_____

_____

_____

_____

_____

_____

_____

_____

_____

_____

_____

_____

_____

CHAPTER 4

APRIL- APRIL SHOWERS BRING MAY FLOWERS, PRAISES GO UP, SO THE BLESSINGS RAIN DOWN.

*"No rain, no rainbow!
No rain, no flowers!"*

In this chapter we focus on having the intestinal fortitude, the strong backbone, and the indomitable will to push forward in the face of challenges and the storms of life! I know that through every storm in my life where I was able to persevere, keep the faith, and keep my praises going up, the blessings rain down! And also metaphorically speaking, there's been a beautiful rainbow at the end of the storm. So in this section of our VIP program, I'm going to train you to always see the silver lining of the grey rain clouds!

Let's get real here - life is not a fairytale. Life is tough. Life has challenges. Life is unfair. Life will kick you down so hard and sometimes you think you might not be able to get up. Well I'm here to tell you if you can get up, and show up, and never give up – you will have the victory!

In this book you are going to learn so many timeless universal life hacks, tools, tips, and techniques that are going to help you to crack your success code!

PRAISE

You got to praise it up so the blessings come down! When you're constantly using your voice, your mouth as positive tools to trumpet and sound off all of the beautiful things you have to be grateful for, and that you let everyone know you are too blessed to be stressed, you create an impenetrable, invisible, force field of strength and protection around you. It is true! As soon as I wake up I just start going through everything I have to be grateful for. So just my healthy strong mind and body, the roof over my head, the healthy food that I feed my body, and plus the positive thoughts that I choose to think daily.

When the praises go up it's true that the miracles rain down. So keep praising it up!

PRAYER

In one of my many interviews, the interviewer asked me what was my favorite exercise. They were expecting me to say squats, ab crunches, or bicep curls. But my answer was prayer. Prayer is my most powerful and favorite daily exercise. It transforms the entire day. It transforms bad to good, weak to strong, and negative to positive.

Battles are won not by standing up screaming and yelling. But battles are worn on your knees in silent prayer to your Higher Power. You see, prayer is the next level of praise. Praise is when you openly and publicly share your praises of what you're so grateful for. Prayer, on the other hand, is when you go behind closed doors, and you strongly make a plea to God for support, clarity, guidance, protection, calling upon divine intervention, the Holy Spirit, to give you the strength, the determination, the discipline, and the support that you need to battle and win your daily challenges. And with God, you will always come out with the victory!

Prayer is extremely powerful, not only because you are praising your Higher Power. But more importantly it is outright warfare on the enemy. When you put the enemy on notice, and you've declared to yourself and your higher power that you will not be a victim, but you will be victorious - you've already won the battle.

GRATITUDE

Practicing gratitude is essential to reclaiming and unleashing your VIP power. From reading my first book, you realize the importance I put on this daily ritual. However in this sequel, we're going to kick it up a notch. In positive psychology research, gratitude is strongly and consistently associated with greater happiness. Gratitude helps people feel more positive emotions, truly enjoy a good experience on another level, improve their health, deal with adversity, and build strong relationships. Even Harvard Health has been shown that giving things can make you happier. The benefits are endless! Don't take my word for it. Research reveals gratitude can have these benefits.

1. Grateful people sleep better.

3. Gratitude improves self-esteem.

4. Gratitude opens the door to better quality relationships.

5. Gratitude improves physical health.

6. When you practice gratitude it decreases aggression and increases empathy.

7. When you're grateful, you actually improve your physical health.

You're probably thinking, "okay Coach JNL, I get it. Gratitude works. But how can I actually practice being more grateful? I have a hard time getting out of this funk and I want to hold a grudge and I want to be better but I know that being grateful will actually help me what are my first steps?"

Here's some great steps to help you become more grateful, that are actual exercises to help you increase your gratitude. Think of gratitude as a muscle - the more you use it, the stronger it'll get!

1. Watch your language. What you talk about, you bring about. If you talk about how grateful you are for your strong healthy mind and body and this beautiful day that you have, and the roof of your head and the healthy food to get to eat, you will increase more of that. Instead of rambling on and complaining about what you don't like, flip it and empower your life through the language of gratitude.

2. Remember the bad times in your life. It sounds counterproductive, but it's actually very healing and helpful. This is a powerful "tool to pick out of your gratitude toolbox" when you're feeling a little bit down. Simply remembering the bad times in your life, and how you were able to get through them, will give you a sense of victory and also gratitude. So reflect on the past bad memories and give yourself a pat on the back, assuring yourself that you can and will get through whatever situation you're facing. This will give you the seed of gratitude in that moment that will help you see your current situation in better positive light.

3. Learn some prayers of gratitude. In many spiritual traditions, prayers of gratitude are considered to be the most powerful form of prayer. Why? Because through these prayers people recognize the "Ultimate Source of All",

which sheds light on just how minor our current worries and troubles are.

4. Use the power of contrast to create more gratitude. When feeling ungrateful, use the power of contrast to quickly shift into being grateful. How? Think how other people who are sick, dealing with terminal illness, or having to lay a loved one to rest, or someone who filed for bankruptcy, or someone who lost a limb, or who was in a horrifying accident that was life threatening or left them in a very bad physical situation, you will quickly see just how much you have to be grateful for.

5. Keep a gratitude journal. There's a power in writing or typing. When you write something on paper or type something, it fortifies and solidifies all the things that you have to be grateful for, such as your gifts, your benefits, and all the good things you enjoy daily. When you set aside the time everyday to think back of beautiful memories of gratitude that are also associated with ordinary everyday events, you make your ordinary days extraordinary, and that is a miracle in itself

<u>VISION</u>

I use the power of visualization in times of uncertainty. Just like it says in the Bible in Proverbs 29:18 'where there is no vision, the people perish." you must have a vision of what you want to achieve, and of your dream life. Even times that are harsh and bleak, this is where the power of visualization and having a vision come into play. Just like affirmations are beneficial for motivation, focus, and effective goal-setting, so too is visualization or what I like to call as mental imagery.

You might think that people have only been using the power of visualizations since the 70s and 80s when the self-help gurus started to surface. But humans have been visualizing for years, ever since creation, since the beginning of time. Whenever we have an idea or want to create a new project, we must visualize it first. Even for our basic instincts, if we're hungry and we want to eat something, we picture different food possibilities. And advertisers have hacked into our visualization power by teasing us and taunting us with appealing visuals of food, that trigger an internal hunger that can only be satiated by eating that food. So we must be very careful with the power of having a vision and using visualization techniques.

What is visualization? Is the use of imagination through pictures or mental imagery to create visions of what we want in our lives and how we make them happen. Along with focus and emotional becomes a powerful, creative tool that helps us achieve what we want in life. Used correctly it can bring about self-improvement, maintain great health, help you perform well in your fitness and fat loss efforts, and help you accomplish all goals in your life.

As your coach, I use mental imagery to help you envision yourself performing the workout first and then actually physically executing it. I coach you to visualize yourself doing a squat, burpee, ab crunch, jumping jack, or any cardio bursts . You must first see it in your mind before you can actually physically do it.

FUNWORK: I want you to actually take the time to perform or rehearse an event or the dream life that you want to live, or maybe visualize living in your dream home in your mind. Whatever you want to manifest, see it in your mind in vivid color, as you will create the neural patterns to teach your muscles in your mindset to do exactly what you want them to do!

PERSISTENCE In the game of weight loss, success, life, and everything worth fighting for, you must be persistent. Without persistence, your ability to grow and develop as a person will be severely restricted, and so will be the amount of success, wealth, and happiness that you will be able to achieve. So what's my point? DON'T GIVE UP!

And let's face it. Life is full of challenges. No matter what you do in your life, there will always be times when things don't go according to plan, times when everything seems to be working against you, and times when you will fail. But remember, there's no such thing as failure, only results! These results tell you what to do better next time.

And at moments like these when you feel like giving up, you may even have a decreased sense of confidence and lowered self-esteem that makes you feel bad about yourself. The easy thing to do during such times is to quit what we are doing, give up, throw in the towel, and move on to something else. Its common that we choose something that's easier or distracts us from our previous goals. This is where failure comes in. To give up too soon is a failure. That's why I always say never give up!

Humans are wired to do the things that are fun and easy over those that are hard and necessary. This is exactly why the large majority of people in our society settle and never fight for their dreams.

You, as a VIP, are one of the chosen few who keep going through periods of adversity, and therefore you have a solid chance of achieving something of real meaning and value in your life. We as VIPs don't focus on being perfect. However we focus on being persistent. Being persistent will make you much more likely to achieve your hopes and dreams.

So here are my top tips on how to become more persistent and stop focusing on the end result. Let's focus on enjoying the journey, and not the destination.

1. Do it Because You Love It: Workout because you love it. Eat clean because you love it, not because you want to lose weight, or see a certain number on the scale. Shift your focus from obsessing

getting there, to being in the moment. Redirect your attention on lifelong characteristics and habits that will keep you healthy forever, not a quick fix.

2. Remember your why. Your why needs to be strong. Why do you want to get in shape? It can't be something frivolous like wanting to look good in a bikini. It must be something serious like to truly get your health in order, to fight off a chronic disease, or fight off an illness. Or to be strong for your children. Finding out your why, will help you identify and nurture your motivation. If you know why you're doing what you're doing, it gives you more energy to keep moving.

3. Outline your definite action steps and be consistent! When you know how to get what you want it makes it easier to achieve it. To know how, do some research and planning of what needs to be done your part. Be specific on each step you need to take.

4. Support. It's been proven that those who have support from a coach and a community of like-minded individuals will be that much more likely to stick with it, be consistent, keep your eye on the prize, and never give up.

5. Last but not least, you must keep a positive mental attitude. The road to success is not easy. In fact, it's very challenging, and this is why only

few succeed. There will be countless times when you'll be faced with defeat and if you are weak, you'll be succumbing to negative thoughts of fears, doubts and will eventually give up. Regardless of the situation, in order to develop persistence and to succeed in crushing your goals, a VIP must always maintain a positive mental attitude, or PMA for short. Keep your thoughts focused on taking action towards your goal. Avoid negative thoughts at all costs, as it will ruin your concentration and persistence.

RESILIENCE

Resilience is the capacity to recover quickly from difficulties. Psychologists define resilience as the process of adapting well in the face of adversity, trauma, tragedy, threats, or significant sources of stress, such as family and relationship problems, serious health problems, or financial stressors. Sadly enough a lot of us do not have the resilience we need in order to pursue and crush our goals and dreams.

I'm going to be honest with you. If any of you have read any of my past books, many of you know that I have a tremendous amount of resilience. How did I gain all this resilience? Through life itself. From my bleak childhood, from the challenges I faced at a very young age, having to fend for myself, and being forced to bounce back after tremendous setbacks. Even though these difficulties were extremely hard at the time, I look back now and I'm very grateful for them. Life does not hand us a map, we will all experience twists and turns, from every day challenges, to traumatic events, with more lasting impact, and each change affects people differently. But here I am is your VIP life coach, telling you that you can bounce back stronger after facing life changing situations in stressful situations from nurturing your resilience.

Increasing your resilience is like building a muscle. It takes time and intention. I want you to focus on the four VIP core components that will help you build your resilience.

1. Self-care/Your VIP Wellness Program: Self-care maybe a popular buzzword, but it is essential for you to practice it daily in order for you to have stable mental health and therefore build resilience. That's because stress is just as much physical as it is emotional. Self-care is a legitimate practice for those who want to promote positive lifestyle factors such as proper nutrition, getting sufficient sleep, staying hydrated, exercising regularly, which strengthens your body and helps you adapt to stress and reduces anxiety or depression.

2. Support/Connect with Like Minded People/Groups: VIPs, we must prioritize our relationships! Connecting with empathetic

people who we can trust, who are there to support us, and also remind us that we are not alone in all of life's challenges, will help us build resiliency. Focus on seeking out honest and kind individuals who validate your feelings, which will support you, your efforts, and in the time of need be there for you. Sometimes the pain of real life's challenges or even traumatic events can cause some people to isolate themselves, but I am here as your transformational coach to remind you that it's important to accept help and support from those who care about you.

Treat finding high-quality people as if it was your profession. This is a job. Prioritize genuinely connecting with people who care about you. Reclaim your hope in humanity by joining a group. This is why I created the VIP coaching program. Along with one-on-one relationships, some people find that being active in groups, or faith-based online communities, provides the social support that can help you be more resilient. If you're not a member of our www.JNLVIP.com Online Coaching program, I highly suggest that you do join as you will increase your resilience by being around supportive, kind, and compassionate women who have your back and are rooting for your success.

3. Be Mindful: Being aware and enlightened will also help you increase being resilient. Mindful journaling, mindful movement such as yoga or deep detox stretching, or spiritual practices like prayer can help you build connections that restore hope, and also help you deal with situations that require resilience. When you practice mindful movement, write, pray, meditate, journal, or ruminate on positive aspects of your life and remember the things that you're grateful for, even during personal trials, you will be building your muscles of resiliency.

4. Don't Mask Your Pain: Avoid negative outlets such as numbing your pain with alcohol, drugs, or other substances, because it's like putting a bandage on a deep wound. Instead shift your focus on giving your body resources to manage stress, rather than seeking to eliminate the feeling of stress altogether. To be honest with you, when you drink alcohol or do drugs, you're only making the situation worse and getting into a deep black hole that will be very hard to get out of. Emotionally eating, or even abusing a loved one, as sometimes we take out are negative energy on those closest to us, are not smart ways to deal with stress. You're only hurting yourself and your loved ones. Instead transition your energy from hurt to healing. It's all about healing yourself, and if you go back to step number one with self-care,

you will be able to truly crack your resilience code.

5. Take the Blame: Okay I know this sounds unfair. But it's a creative way for me to express how we must be proactive in accepting our emotions during hard times. We must encourage self-discovery by asking ourselves questions such as "What can I do about this problem in my life", or "How did I attract this problem into my life?" or "How am I helping to bring this problem into my life." For example, when I was younger, and just started working in my late teenager years, I got fired from work one time and it really hurt. I knew I wasn't able to convince my boss it was a mistake to let me go. But instead I took the initiative and became proactive. I spent an hour each day developing my top strengths and started working on my resume. I took the situation by the horns and made a decision that I will never be fired or let go again. I summoned up the motivation I needed and found a purpose even during the stressful time of my life. So I urge you to self-reflect and to create a list of constructive criticisms of yourself that will help you rise up during these painful times of your life.

6. Use the Power of Contrast: I love this VIP principal! It's extremely powerful. It's similar to "Flipping It", but in this VIP technique, instead of

flipping it a 180, we flip it on the opposite side of the spectrum, finding an extreme case to compare against our situation. No matter how bad we have it, there's someone out there in the world that has it 1,000 times worse than us! If we keep that powerful thought of contrast in mind, we will always keep a level head and be more resilient and bounce back. I use this whenever I find myself feeling overwhelmed. I remind myself that what happened to me is an indicator of how my future will be, and that I'm not helpless. And someone else out there has it 1,000 times worse than me. I know I might not be able to change a highly stressful event, but I can change how I interpret it and also respond to it.

7. Learn From Your Past: This is a powerful VIP tool where you look back at who or what was helpful in previous times of distress, and this will help you discover how you can respond effectively to new difficult situations in the future. You must constantly remind yourself that where have you been able to find the strength and ask yourself what you've learned from those past experiences. Just take a quick 60 seconds and look back at some of the darkest and bleakest moments of your life. Look how you bounced back! Look how you made it! Look how you only became stronger from the situation!

In closing, repeat three times "I am resilient! I am strong! Nothing will ever stop me from being the best person I can be! I am a VIP!

ADAPTABILITY

A VIP woman always adapts. She is always flexible while keeping her eye on the prize.

There's so many benefits to being adaptable. Being adaptable is a skill set that a VIP woman must master. It means working without boundaries, living your best life, being open to finding diverse and unexpected solutions to problems in everyday challenges. A VIP woman has never met a challenge she didn't like, and she kicks that challenge to the curb!

A VIP woman is always looking for new ways of handling multiple tasks and tolerating external pressure. She always remains composed even when faced with ambiguity or any kind of emergency. She daily cracks her code by learning new tricks, tips, and techniques that will help build her confidence up when dealing with different types of people, different situations, or whatever life throws at her.

Have you ever met that woman, pardon the terminology, but always "gets her panties in a wad"? She always gets flustered when things don't go according to plan. She allows herself to get frustrated, and then she goes off on a ranting rampage, wasting time and energy. To me, this is nonsense. As a transformational coach, I know I should have a little more patience with women like this. Especially when they're over the age of 25. We should know by then that nothing ever goes as planned. We must always remain composed, poised, and exude grace in times of pressure and when situations go into limbo land. You must control the situation, and not let the situation control you. A woman who cannot adapt to the ever-evolving changes of every situation will only self-sabotage herself. A woman who adapts will succeed. There will be countless times we experience unexpected unpleasant situations in life. Being adaptable insures you stay afloat when adversities of life try to sink you down.

And we all know that stress can kill. If you are adaptable, you will have less stress. Learning how to manage change with a positive upbeat attitude will decrease your stress and increase your success.

Being adaptable will help you stand strong in every hopeless situation that arise from time to time. Once you are confident that you have all it takes to begin the change process right within you, you will have unlocked more happiness for yourself.

When you are adaptable you will bounce back that much stronger whenever life knocks you down. We as VIPs must embrace and flow with change, instead of running away from it. Adaptable people are resilient. And from countless case studies, clients, and coaching consultations, I am convinced that an individuals success isn't dependent on their level of education, or how much experience they have or even their intelligence. It is their level of resilience that really matters. In this section, I am going to go over the "must-do's" in order to become more adaptable, which is a large gemstone in a VIP woman's crown.

There are certain key ingredients to becoming more adaptable. They are listed below.

Willingness: A VIP woman always shows willingness to learn new skills that increase efficiency and her being more effective, always working on herself.

Hard Work: She must also have a deep willingness to work longer and harder. When a woman works hard, she is free to admire her own willingness to work extra hours in order to "show up for' what she needs to take care of. And I have learned time and time again that nothing trumps hard work. Tip: once you start a task, go ahead and already accept that it will be "hard work", so if any hiccups occur, you won't be emotionally side-swiped, but instead, if the task is easy, you will feel over-accomplished and ready to keep "swinging hard" at your workload.

Acceptance: She always works on accepting all types of change positively and handles changing workloads in response to ever evolving circumstances. I never get stressed and I learned to embrace mishaps with renewed energy and vigor. Those that allow their emotions to get entangled in a spiderweb, seem to never get out. You must stay above the fray.

SURVIVAL OF THE FITTEST

We live in a dog-eat-dog world. Women tend to be emotional by design, which is fine because we are the nurturers, the home caretakers, and our loving towards our children and loved ones. However, it can also backfire on us. When we are mistreated, overlooked, overworked, underpaid, we may get off-kilter and go down and emotional downward spiral, leaving us not in control. This is where adaptability comes into play with "Survival of the Fittest".

My Intentions and goals for all of my clients worldwide are for you to get stronger, and evolve everyday. Therefore, it is safe to say that a VIP woman will always get stronger when engaged in our JNL VIP Program Online. She gets stronger mentally, emotionally, physically, and spiritually. Even though the term survival of the fittest originated from Darwinian Evolution theory of the way of describing the mechanism of natural selection, I like to use it here to describe how a VIP woman will always be at the top of her game because I will be challenging her to get stronger in all areas of her life.

Some of the programs actually make you weaker and cause you to de-evolve. I'm here to help you evolve and get on an upward spiral, reaching new heights of success everyday. As your coach, how do I do this? By always challenging you! I will always give you workouts that are hard. I will always be pushing you to do more, try more, and achieve more. I will always make sure you're not settling for playing victim to life's hardships, but conquering all that you do and coming out victorious.

FUN WORK: To wrap up this chapter, I want you to write below how you are going to become more persistent, resilient, adaptable, and become stronger:

_____

_____

_____

_____

_____

_____

_____

_____

_____

_____

NOTES FOR CHAPTER 4:

_____

_____

_____

_____

_____

_____

_____

_____

_____

_____

_____

_____

_____

_____

_____

_____

_____

_____

CHAPTER 5

MAY FLOWERS- MAY IS THE MONTH OF MANIFESTING MIRACLES

"You, reading this right now, are a miracle!
-Jennifer Nicole Lee

This is going to be an extremely powerful month! The next 30 days we are going to celebrate manifesting miracles. I'm going to coach you on how to become a powerful manifestor beyond your wildest dreams. Because, yes, thoughts become things. What you think about, you bring about. What you talk about, you bring about. Where your focus goes, energy flows.

As a transformational coach, it is essential for me to teach you to become a powerful manifestor of miracles. Why? Well you are a ceator. You are co-creating with the universe. You don't receive any miracles from others. You create it. You attract it. You believe it. You see it. You receive it! Once you understand this shift in paradigm, there are no limits to what you can do.

Sadly enough we were all raised that whatever we want lies outside of us. Someone else has our gifts. Someone else has our way to our goals. Someone else will grant us the right and the authority to receive what is our hearts desire. These are all myths. It all starts with you. In this chapter you are going to crack the miracle code, and start manifesting your hopes, dreams, and aspirations. And yes, it will be fun!

In chapter one, for New Year New You, we learned how to visualize and work with a vision board. Now since you made it through the program a couple of months, or even if this is a few years into the program, we are going to kick it up a notch and become master manifestor.

You will get to the point where you don't even need a vision board, or a vision journal, or even needing to write your miracles down that you want to manifest. You're going to become such a strong manifestor, that you think it, and it will come into fruition, manifesting in the very near future. But it takes time, practice, skill, and faith.

FAITH: why is faith so important to manifesting miracles? Because it is the foundation, the cement slab if you will, of the beginning of miracles. Faith is the seed of a miracle. You are not able to manifest a miracle in your life without having faith. This is the number one stumbling block for many people who say they cannot manifest.

Faith is the complete trust or confidence in something knowing that even though you might not see it physically, you know that it exists and it is there. Faith is believing beyond a shadow of a doubt that your higher power is at work for you. Having faith means knowing your Miracle will come into fruition, even when you don't even see a possible way.

HOW TO INCREASE YOUR FAITH:

We must learn how to increase our faith in order to manifest miracles. Are my top ways to increase our faith so we may become powerful manifestors.

<u>Pray</u>- A powerful way to increase your faith is to pray. When you go into prayer asking to have your faith strengthened, it will be so! God said that blessed are those who have not seen yet still believe. Yet I know with life, challenges, trials, and tribulations, sometimes we doubt and refuse to believe unless we're able to touch it and see it. If we go in prayer and ask to have our faith strengthened, it's amazing how our faith will actually be increased.

<u>Meditate</u>: Meditation is essential to increasing your faith. Fear is the opposite of faith. If we fail to stop and meditate, fear can override our emotions, triggering anxiety, depression, and a sense of hopelessness. Once we meditate, and mentally flip the fear into faith, we are mentally and emotionally stronger. This increases our faith.

Visualize: As you know by now the powerful tool of visualization is weaved all throughout the VIP program. Many of our well-seasoned VIP members use this technique in so many capacities. And yes you can use it to increase your faith. Even on your darkest and hardest days, evoke the power of visualization seeing yourself manifesting the miracle you want to happen. Whether it's a sick loved one, whether you're going through a chronic illness, or financial hardship, visualize yourself being healed, whole, and coming out of this challenging situation victorious.

Don't Listen to Negative People: There's a phenomenon that happens once a VIP woman reclaims and unleashes her VIP power. Yes, you guessed it, negative people come out of the woodwork. This is where your faith has to kick in. You're going to hear negative comments from everybody telling you how it's not going to work, stop dreaming, don't waste your time, and that you are delusional. You must remain steadfast in your goals and focus the miracles you want to manifest. Don't let their negative vibes taint your focus. And in true VIP style, flip it and use their negativity to fuel your faith.

Don't Try to Convince the Non-believers: The enemy will come at you at many different angles, and many different activities and forms. Once you know just how strong your VIP power is, the enemy will come to challenge you. They will bring fear attempting to crush your faith. Your initial reaction is to convince them. Don't do this. This will only exhaust you. You must maintain all of your faculties and energy to manifest your miracles. Using your energy to attempt to convince those that don't believe in you, will only drain you of your much-needed energy for your faith. Instead, don't waste your energy on convincing non-believers, and pour that energy and focus into your faith. In short, starve the non-believers and feed your faith.

<u>Listen to Your Higher Power:</u> Learning to lean into and listen to your higher power is essential to increasing your faith. Cultivate this relationship between you and your higher power. It is sacred and powerful. Don't you know that your higher power is listening to you, guiding you, and showing you the way? You know that you were never alone, therefore you should never leave your life in fear, but rather in extreme faith.

<u>Forgive:</u> I know it might be hard to forgive others for their wrong doings towards you. But once you forgive, the gift is not for them, it is actually for you. Hanging onto resentment is like holding onto a hot coal, with the intentions of burning the wrong door. But you're only burning yourself. Therefore make a list of everyone you need to forgive, and release them out of your energy field. Once you release these negative emotions out of your energy field, you will now free up the space in your spirit to receive the miracles that you are worthy of. When you forgive others, it's like removing the roadblocks and

barricades that are stopping the miracles from coming to you.

<u>Accept God's healing:</u> In life we all get hurt. We get injured emotionally, physically, and mentally. But once you accept God's healing energy into your life, you increase your faith. But you must be willing and available to receive His healing. Once you declare personally that you are ready, willing, and able to receive all of God's love for you, the miracle "faucet" will be turned on.

<u>Don't Rely on Reasoning</u>: We as human beings want to rationalize everything. But this is where we stall our miracle successes. We must not rely on reason, but divine intervention, having faith that there is a higher power at work here, beyond human understanding and human capability.

<u>WHAT IS A MIRACLE?</u> Before we move on, let's get clear on what a miracle is. Many believe in Miracle is a unicorn flying across the sky, or a big bag of money falling down right on top of your head. These are not miracles! And actually, miracles happen every day. It's when you open up your eyes, it's when you wake up to have another day. A miracle is when you're able to see your family and tell them that you love them. A miracle is when you're able to donate to a charity, even if it is a small amount, knowing that you are putting miracles into motion in other people's lives. A miracle is having clarity on what your goals are and what you want to achieve in

life. And miracle is healing energy bestowed upon your life, from years of resentment, confusion, and anger. A miracle is when someone is finally ready to take full responsibility of their life and stop blaming others. A miracle happens when someone has finally hit rock bottom for the last time, and they will do everything in their power to create a healthy, happy, and balanced life for themselves. Once you see a miracle as an everyday event, you're able to build the momentum, and create bigger miracles that you want to manifest.

ASK, AND YOU SHALL RECEIVE

One of the most profound ways of creating and manifesting miracles in your life can be found in Matthew Chapter 7 Verses 6-8.

> "Do not give dogs what is holy; do not throw your pearls before swine. If you do, they may trample them under their feet, and then turn and tear you to pieces._Ask_and_it will be given_to you;_seek and_you will find;_knock_and_the door will be opened_to you. For everyone who asks receives; he who seeks finds; and to him who knocks, the door will be opened."

So keep looking, keep knocking, and get ready for the doors of your miracles to be opened!

ASK, BELIEVE AND RECEIVE

Moving on to the next practical way for you to create miracles in your life is to ask, believe, and receive. This is another way of expressing "ask and you shall receive".

This method has been popularized by the book and movie "The Secret".

Ask, believe, receive is the Law of Attraction's motto. It's very simple, yet very profound. From my experience, the first step of asking is the easiest. Ask for what you want. It's that simple. Many of us can do that. But when we go on to the next two steps this is where we get tripped up.

The next two steps of believing and receiving can be difficult or a challenge to the person who wants to manifest a miracle. Sometimes it's the believing part that trips most people up. Believing can be hard, because we have to believe in the unseen in order to get what we want. This is why I covered the subject of faith, believing in the unseen. So "flex your faith muscles" here in step 2.

The last and most important step in my experience is the most difficult out of these two steps. We all can ask, we all can believe to some extent, but secretly we feel deep down inside we are not worthy of receiving. Many of us deal with guilt and shame for receiving gifts or what we want. In the past when we've gotten our way, other people made us feel bad about it. When things are really going your way, there always seems to be one jealous or envious person who attempts to mess everything up. So how do we push through? We must retrain ourselves to know that we are worthy and deserving.

So repeat after me three times the following statement below that will help you unlock your receiving potential:

> I am deserving and worthy of receiving my greatest good.
>
> I am deserving and worthy of receiving my greatest good.
>
> I am deserving and worthy of receiving my greatest good.

Become more aware of when you are blocking your own miracles. For instance, maybe you are blocking your miracles because you secretly and subconsciously don't want those around you to be jealous of you.

In addition many of us have a hard time dealing with unwanted attention. Once you receive your miracles, people will notice. We must get comfortable with others noticing the greatness in our lives. It comes with the territory of receiving miracles and being blessed. So this is where we flip it. Once you start seeing others noticing your miracles, this is a good sign to keep manifesting! Don't shrink, don't wish it away, and don't stop your Miracles! Push through! You will find those negative energy vampires who drain you, or want to throw a wrench into your miracle wheel. Then the angels will also be flushed out, coming to celebrate your success. This is an important crossroads in cultivating and growing your VIP power. You must let go of the energy vampires while embracing the angels in your life.

LET'S GET CLEAR:

Write in the space below the miracles you would like to manifest! There's no right or wrong! This is your time to dream and dream big!

_____

_____

_____

_____

_____

_____

_____

_____

_____

_____

_____

Now that we are clear, let's move onto the next steps of manifesting your miracles into existence:

Clear space: In order for you to be ready, willing and able to receive the miracles you want to manifest, you must stay open for signs and opportunities from the universe and show up for these assignments that are brought to you.

Universal assignments come in many different opportunities. Maybe you're guided to a job that will bring up some of your weaknesses that you need to work on. Maybe you'll be led to a relationship that will conjure up all of your past problems so you have to finally heal yourself and get rid of all fear that is still lingering around. Even though this is a painful process, you must trust that these Universal assignments are essential steps for you to clean your energy, and also incredible opportunities to clear the space in order for you to receive your next round of miracles.

Feel It: Do you remember these memories? Your first kiss. When you became a mother. Losing your first pet. Your wedding day. Your divorce. Your first heartbreak. The first time you experienced death. Graduations. Getting fired. Getting hired. I could go on and on. These are all strong emotions. They are not only stored in our memories, but they are stored in the cells of our bodies. We hold on to them, carrying this mental load around with us all day and they begin to play over and over again and the background of our lives. And when we hold onto these memories, experiences and feelings. And then they shape our future. But guess what! We can harness this powerful technique and actually change the direction of our lives by creating the miracles we seek by linking emotion to them.

Linking an emotion to the miracle you want to attract is a powerful manifesting technique. Once you become clear on your intention, spend some time every day to focus your energy of feeling what it is that you want to manifest. First think about your miracle in your mind. Then let the feeling flow from your mind down into your body taking over all of your energy. The stronger you feel the faster it is on its way.

Chill: Set your intention out to the universe. Visualize. Know you've already received your miracle. And let go. This is a hard part for many because humans are wired to be control freaks. But we must trust and let go. In other words, chill! God knows the right time. The universe knows what it is doing! So do your part, by doing nothing, but believing, having faith, and putting the control factor into the hands of God and the universe.

Be the opposite of Paranoid: we've all heard about being paranoid. But what really is it? Paranoia is an instinct or thought process which is believed to be heavily influenced by anxiety and fear often to the point of delusion and irrationality. Paranoid thinking typically includes beliefs of conspiracy concerning perceived threat towards oneself. Someone who suffers from paranoia believes as if everyone is out to get them.

So why don't we ever hear about the opposite of being paranoid! I dug deep and found that there actually is a state that is the exact opposite of being paranoid. It is called pronoia. Paranoia is a state of mind that is the exact and complete opposite of paranoia. For instance, a person suffering from paranoia feels that people are the world are conspiring against them, where a person experiencing pronoia feels that the world around them is actually conspiring to do them good! So be pronoia, and not paranoid! Know that the universe is working in your honor. Know that people are in your life to help and support you. Know that everything that happens to you, even though it may seem bad at first, has a hidden message or gift that will help you along your journey in a positive way. Everything that happens to you in your life has a life lesson in it, and it comes with a gift! It is up to us to choose to see the world in a positive way!

Stay Committed to Happiness and Joy: Its simple. When you are happy and radiating joy, you naturally attract more miracles in your life. Make it a conscious decision to be happy right when you wake up. How can you start being happy and joyous? As soon as your eyes open up, go into an attitude of gratitude. This leads me to the next point!

Be Grateful: Choosing to be grateful is a decision. I always get myself into an attitude of gratitude right when I wake up, as it sets the tone for the entire day. And why be miserable? It's like shaking hands with the devil. And a VIP woman never shakes hands with the devil. When you're miserable you're actually telling God that your life is not good enough. That you're unhappy with what he gave you. For me being miserable and ungrateful is a blasphemy. Being ungrateful is extremely dangerous. Why? Because you're actually attracting more things to be ungrateful and miserable about. So flip it, and turn on your gratitude switch!

Become a Vibrational Match. One major VIP key to manifesting anything in life is to become a vibrational match to it by practicing the desired emotion of what it is that you want. First, feel and truly embody that emotion, and then the desired manifestation has to come! Once you've got all your beliefs lined up, the next step is to become a vibrational match to what it is that you want. So how do you do this? It's extremely basic, but potent.

As a VIP woman you can attest to just how strong your thoughts are. It is safe to say what you think about you bring about. Your thoughts pretty much basically create your reality. So you're attracting what you're thinking about all day which then shows up in your life. For example, if you're thinking about just how poor you are, you will continue to attract living in lack and scarcity. If you think about how unsuccessful you are, you will not accomplish any goals. That's why I am constantly flipping it! So instead of focusing on how poor you are, focus on how abundant you are, become the vibrational match of what you want to attract! And there is no hoping! Hoping is a weak and impotent emotion coming from a place of uncertainty. You will attract chaos. I mean, look around you, there's no shortage of women that are living in chaos, attracting more hot messes their way!

Let's take it a step further. If you become the vibrational match of being wealthy, by knowing you're wealthy, by believing without a shadow of a doubt that you are wealthy, and being convinced with clarity with emotions that resonate with abundance, you will attract wealth. On the other hand if you think about becoming wealthy in the future, you will continue to attract scarcity and living in lack. Why? Because if you are hoping to attract wealth, then you are affirming that you don't currently have it. And if you continue to vibrate on that level of not having wealth but and wanting it you will continue not to be wealthy and continue to want it.

This scenario is exactly the same with your health. If you're constantly focusing on how unhealthy and how weak you are, you will continue to attract all of that. However if you shift your focus, and transition your thoughts, energy, and emotions from zeroing in on what an unhealthy life you live, to what a super healthy and high vibrational life you live, this shift will give you the energy to take immediate action and will create the dream healthy life that you deserve to live. It all starts with your thoughts, so become a vibrational match this very instant to what you want to achieve.

A VIP woman does not wish for what she wants, rather she works for it. Erroneously, many people believe that wishing for something will make it appear in their life. When you wish for something, or hope or something, or try to get something, or maybe something will happen, and that you "kind of sort of want" in your life will appear, the universe brings you more of that - confusion and chaos. Instead, you must know it, feel it, see it, and believe it with crystal clear clarity!

Receive it already: I love to use this practice as it changes your results in advance. Already see yourself as having received your miracle that you want to manifest. It is already here. It is already happening. You have received it now. Instant manifestations will become a daily occurrence for you, when you're not contradicting your own vibrational desires. So you have to Quantum Leap your results in advance, fast forward into the future to see, believe, and accept that you've already received your miracle. This collapses time space, and forces your miracles to manifest quicker, with more ease, and less struggle.

Last but not least, my favorite part of this section - it's all about fun, fun, fun!

Make Manifesting Miracles Fun: manifesting is fun. Don't make it stressful. Don't make it hard. This is where you stall and stop your success and results. Remove resistant thought and action from your desire. What does this mean? Resistance thought is simply a habit of thought that is different from your desire. If you like to try a new workout move, but it's so far outside your comfort zone you might link struggle, pain, and discomfort to this desire. If you want to make more money, but you associate making more money in your profession as hard and nearly impossible, you've already put your brakes on it. Your put a K on the end of that word fun and you put yourself into a funk!

When you no longer split your energy flow with contradicting thoughts you will know your VIP power and it becomes so much fun!

The reason why you're not attracting your miracles, is that you secretly and subconsciously associate pain, discomfort, hardship, and struggle. Many of us subconsciously feel that actually having your miracles come into reality as being uncomfortable. What would your family think? Would it upset your family? Would you make your friends jealous? Would not everyone be happy for you? What would your parents think of you? Would your soulmate become intimidated by all the blessings coming your way? I can go on and on. We must flush this immediately as we will only be doing the

"Texas two-step" and be taking two steps forward, then two steps back, only to find yourself in the same place.

To close out this section of our VIP book on how to manifest miracles, please select any of your favorite tools tips techniques on how to crack your miracle code. Use the space below to take any notes to refer back to. This is where the fun begins! Now let's manifest your miracles!

_____

_____

_____

_____

_____

_____

_____

_____

_____

_____

_____

_____

_____

MAY FLOWERS:

The theme of May is "April showers bring May flowers." This is a powerful metaphor symbolizing that if you're able to weather the storms of life, you will come out smelling like a rose!

But how do we weather the storms of life? Here's some simple steps that will help you to see the rainbow after the rains have stopped!

1. Expect the storms of life. Knowing that they will come, you will be prepared. And if you're prepared, you will survive them. You'll be ready to weather them by keeping your anchor dug deep, allowing you to have control, clarity, comfort, and calmness in the middle of chaos.

2. Lean on your higher power, lean on your VIP friends, and lean on your coach! I am here for you! It's sad but it's true. When life is going great, everyone's your friend. When life is hard, everybody seems to go "ghost on you" and disappear, and you can hear the sounds of crickets! That's when your real friends are there for you. Don't be afraid to seek support, and a virtual pat on the back from your VIP sisters worldwide. And as you know, as your coach, I'm always here for you!

3. Be Hyper-Responsible: this is where my tough love coach comes out. If you are over the age of

21, you now know firsthand that there are no guarantees in life. You also know that life is not fair. You also know that people are out for themselves, and they are not out to help you. That's the majority. There's 1% of people that I called angels. And when you believe in angels, they appear. These angels are your VIP sisters and your coach. So getting back to you, you have to be hyper responsible, and practice responsibility. When it comes to having to face difficult challenges, it's very common that many of us want to run and avoid them. But it's those VIP victorious champions who weathers life's difficult storms not by running, but instead learning how to practice responsibility. You must be ready to kick butt, with your VIP superhero cape always on, at any given moment. This will shield you from the temptation to wallow in self-pity, victim mentality, or blaming yourself for others. By being hyper responsible, you will be more empowered to find effective solutions that will help you sail the difficult seas of life.

WHAT FLOWER ARE YOU?

Above I mentioned before some powerful techniques to help you weather the storms of life. Now you are in the land of rainbows and endless beautiful fields of flowers! And what flower are you? This is a fun-work activity where you get to spend some time self-reflecting, looking at the qualities that you embody, and celebrating your VIP power! Every May I have our VIP Queens share what type of flower they are, why they connect and identify to that flower, how they are going to continue to nurture and grow this flower, and also what strengths this flower embodies while also looking at its weaknesses, allowing room for more self-growth.

For instance, I myself identify with a sunflower. Sunny, happy, forever pointing its face towards the Sun, with a stiff upright stock that is very strong, which represents a strong backbone and a lot of intestinal fortitude. These flowers are unique in that they have the ability to provide energy in the form of nourishment and vibrancy. Sunflowers represent the sun and the energy provided by its heat and light. The spiritual meaning of sunflower symbolizes faith and that we are always seeking enlightenment and truth.

In the space below please fill out what type of flower you are. Spend some time researching this flower, what it symbolizes, it's spiritual meaning, and also how you are going to continue to nurture and grow this flower, for example by weeding out the weeds, making sure it has plenty of water and nourishment, and keeping away the energy vampires such as bugs, knats, and rodents.

NOTES FOR CHAPTER 5:

_____

_____

_____

_____

_____

_____

_____

_____

_____

_____

_____

_____

_____

_____

_____

_____

_____

CHAPTER 6

JUNE-JUNE IS IN FULL BLOOM WITH JOY! SUMMER, CELEBRATE THE RIPENESS OF LIFE, HALFWAY POINT, REBIRTH & REPOSITION

April Showers brings May Flowers – and now
June is in full bloom!-JNL

June! Oh I love this month! The official month where we end spring, and jump right into Summer! The theme of June is Joy! If we look back at the beginning of the year to January, we all have come such a long way. We've built layers upon layers of our VIP power. Whether you are a new VIP sister, or a veteran VIP, you are now much stronger, focused, and resilient than you were when you started the New Year. This is the halfway point. So I would like to take this month to reflect I'm just how far we've come in six months. We celebrate the ripeness of life! This is an exciting time in your VIP Power journey and evolution-the halfway point through the year, where we celebrate just how far we come, while looking to the second half of the year, carving out goals for the next six months.

June is also my birthday month. So we will be touching upon the theme of birth, and birthing a new higher calling in life. Experiencing a rebirth of mind, body and spirit, pulling from all of the past VIP principles, exercises, fun work, and lessons we learned in the first part of the year.

To me, June represents the ripeness of Summer. All of your hard work of planting and sowing and protecting your seeds, making sure that their roots are deep, and growing in fertile soil, allowing your goals and dreams to grow and manifest.

With all this goal-setting, self-reflection, and manifesting miracles, what is the end result? It truly is to be joyful, to create, have and experience more joy on a deeper level everyday. So as we jump into this new month, celebrating the start of summer, and marking the half part of the year, I will be sharing with you my top VIP tips and how to create more joy in your life.

WHY WE BLOCK OUR OWN JOY: Sadly enough we are the ones who are guilty of blocking our own joy. Subconsciously we feel guilty if we are happy. Even society makes us feel ashamed of being a happy-go-lucky type of person that is positive. They paint us as fool's, with our heads in the clouds, having no grasp of reality. But on the contrary that's the exact opposite. A VIP woman is not a fool, she has her head on her shoulders, and a good firm hold on to reality. She chooses to live a life full of joy.

Society wants those who are happy, joyful, vibrant, and full of life to feel ashamed of our happiness. Why? Because misery loves company. Those who are miserable want other people to be miserable too. But I'm here to tell you as your transformational coach and friend, do not get pulled into their web of negativity. I'm going to teach you in the next section on how to create more joy, have more meaningful happiness in your life, and continue to grow your joy layers upon layers!

Another reason why we block our own joy is that we subconsciously feel that we have to wait for external things to happen in order for us to be joyful. Many of us are overachievers and want to accomplish certain achievements in life, or get to a certain level of success in our profession. You secretly whisper to yourself "once I get that job promotion I'll be happy" or "as soon as I get married I will feel loved and be joyful" or "once I get divorced I can finally feel happy and joyful again". Do you see what happened to you? All of those sayings represented a belief system that you cannot be happy right here and right now for no reason at all. This rule of waiting for something to happen outside of you, in order for you to be happy or experience joy is a terrible and extremely dangerous way to live. You're handing your VIP power to an external experience that may never happen. Reclaim your VIP power, reclaim your joy, and bring it back to you, in your center being, where it belongs. You can create joy inside your mind, body, and spirit just by making the conscious decision to create your own joy every second of the day, starting first thing in the morning right when you open your eyes!

HOW TO CREATE MORE JOY

As I mentioned in the previous paragraph, we must stop waiting to be happy. It's a fact! There are always countless reasons to be joyful. We must shift our focus to notice and appreciate all the reasons we have to be joyful. And no matter what is going on around you, you can feel happier, be productive, and attract success and enjoy yourself during this process. When you shift your focus and the way you mentally process experiences, then your perspective changes. When this powerful shift happens your entire life shifts as well. As I like to say, get your shift together!

You can start being joyful by purposefully and intentionally adding joy to your life right now! The fastest way to experience joy on a daily level, is through you moving your body.

WORKING OUT CREATES MORE JOY:

In the first "Reclaim and Unleash Your VIP Power Book" I went into great detail on how physical movement, exercise, and working out releases dopamine, your brains internal rewards system, rewarding you for taking positive action in your life. This is such a powerful tool to tap into and utilize. When you work out, your body links emotion to motion. When you are doing jumping jacks, burpees, squats, lunges, and any of our VIP signature moves, your body instantaneously goes into a mode of being jolted with joy!

Take my own childhood story for instance. When I was growing up, very poor, with a very bleak and hard childhood, I was riddled with anxiety and fear. I was raised on food stamps, I was teased and bullied as I was a first-generation Italian with immigrant parents, and never fit in and always stood out. Pretty much, life was hell. All that negative energy caused me to go into a downward spiral of worry, anxiety, and depression. I remember distinctly the only time I never felt bad was when I was running, physically playing a sport, exercising, or just moving my body. That distinctly stood out to me. I would wonder why was it that all my worries went away when I was exercising, or playing kickball in the front yard, or playing baseball with the neighborhood kids, or just doing basic jumping jack drills in PE class. It's because my mind was focusing on what your body was doing. I was free for that minute. I link up so much joy to moving my body as it was the only time I had escaped from my everyday worries. That's why I continuously move my body as much as I can on his many days that I can back-to-back. It sets my spirit on fire, and it sets me free. It was my fix for depression. It was my fix for anxiety. It was the non-medicine way without needing a prescription to go to the local pharmacy. And it was actually healthy for me. This is why I linked so much joy to moving my body.

So let's harness the power of movement for increasing the vibrant wellness of our mind body and spirit.

Below is my "VIP Formula" to create an enjoyable balanced wellness program for optimal results.

VIP FORMULA OF WEEKLY MOVEMENT FOR MAX RESULTS

Aim to enjoy 4-6 VIP Workouts per week. No less than four, no more than six.

Go ahead and use your planning day, which usually is Sunday for many of our VIPs, to circle the days you have decided and committed to working out on. And here is a VIP success tip: I always say never miss a Monday! It's the fresh start of the week! And you set the tone for the entire week ahead.

On the days you do not do full length workouts enjoy "Fitness snacks", which could be jumping on your mini-trampoline, going for a brisk walk, enjoying 100 reps of your favorite moves. These "VIP Fitness snacks" will keep your mind body and spirit engaged on your non-training days. I called them active recovery days. And remember, recovery really is the new workout! Your recovery days are just as important as your training days. This is when you actually build and repair your muscles.

As you progress in your VIP program, you're going to truly fall back in love with working out. As your love affair with working out continues, you will see that your admiration for your VIP wellness program and workouts truly unlock your spirit, help you reclaim your VIP power, and you are able to unleash your heart's true desire, to crush your goals, and you will find yourself experiencing a deeper sense of freedom. This leads me to the next chapter all dedicated to freedom, and being independent from anything and everything negative that will hold you back.

CREATING JOY, EXPERIENCING JOY, SEEKING OUT JOY IS ESSENTIAL TO OPTIMAL WELLNESS

As a VIP Queen, you now know that it is your responsibility to daily create your own joy. You create joy through mindful movement, making a conscious decision first thing in the morning to have a joyous day, and to constantly remain in an attitude of gratitude which thus evokes more joy throughout the day. With the mindful movement, the VIP workouts, and you're weekly workout schedule, you will maintain having a joyous spirit, because dopamine is released every time you work out. You are now linking and associating joy and pleasure to working out. Your brain secretes dopamine, the internal reward system, to daily give you a surge of positive energy.

With mindful eating, you then support your workouts with vibrant nutrition, keeping it lean clean and green, as fresh whole foods have been showed to boost one's mood.

Getting off of the fast food, highly processed garbage that only clogged up your energy, and weighed you down, is going to truly increase your sense of well being. You will also decrease your chances of getting sick from diseases and feeling bad after you eat.

And taking care of yourself, is the greatest source of joy ever. Always know that if you allow someone to drain your time, energy, or focus, you are allowing your joy to also deteriorate and wither away. Reclaim your joy by being mindful and guarding your energy, redirecting your focus, and putting an end to all wasted activities and people that only make you regress and not progress in your personal, professional, & physical development.

REBIRTH

June is my birthday month. But I believe every day is our birthday. Another day to be born again, to see life with a new set of eyes. Since this is one of our themes for June, I want you to write down your birthday below:

_____

Now I want you to write the top goals that you must accomplish by the time your next birthday rolls around next year:

_____

_____

_____

_____

_____

_____

_____

_____

_____

_____

_____

_____

_____

_____

_____

_____

_____

_____

_____

_____

_____

_____

Now let's have some birthday fun with all of your goals you wrote above! What are the action steps you need to take in order to manifest, accomplish, and crush these goals by the time your next birthday comes around?

_____

_____

_____

_____

_____

_____

_____

_____

_____

_____

_____

_____

_____

_____

Refer back to your goals that you set, and also your action plan. Just taking the time to write down your goals, reflect on your action plan, and to visualize you already achieving these goals will set you up for success.

With the theme of June being birthdays, it is imperative that you look back at the past six months of this year and celebrate all of your accomplishments! This of course will evoke the emotion of joy and a sense of personal progress.

And after every VIP Workout, you will be flying high! The VIP life is all about love, light, joy, laughter, support, connecting, and vibrating higher! Now this sounds like a daily birthday party to me! As your coach, I'm so grateful for each and everyone of you! And I know many more miracles and success breakthroughs are in the works! I can feel it! I believe it! And we are ready to RECEIVE IT! So congrats on making every day your birthday, a big reason to celebrate!

The time is now, the moment is ripe! Now we move on to the next theme of June-TIMING!

WHEN THE TIME'S RIGHT, THE TIME IS RIPE!
RIPENESS OF THE MOMENT!

All miracles are in God's time. It's our job to name it, claim it, visualize it, believe it, and be ready to receive it. Put all of the right balls into motion. And allow God to show His glory in your life. And yes, timing is everything! While we want things to manifest in our lives quicker, faster, easier, your higher power has a divine timetable for your success.

Having the right timing, and knowing when the time is right, and allowing things to fall into place at the right time are all powerful points in the VIP program.

And having the sense of timing is so important in all areas in life. Think about it. A lot of stress in life comes from poor timing. Either you're in a hurry, or there's a delay, and both of those things can stress you out, being too fast or too slow. One of the keys to success in life is wise timing. And when you do the right thing, at the right time, it just works. On the other hand, can you say the right thing, but at the wrong time, it's a disaster. Also, can you do the right thing, but do it at the wrong time, and it'd be a disaster? Absolutely! Again timing is everything. Comedians must have great timing. Timing is the difference between a good joke and a bad joke. Its the difference between a good leader and a bad leader. Its is not only doing the right thing, but doing it at the right time. Also, a speaker who holds your attention for hours on end, knows the power of timing, while the boring speaker does not.

Think about it, people are paid a lot of money just because they have great timing. A baseball player who knows when to swing his bat at the right time will be paid millions of more dollars that another player whose off by a nanosecond.

So what are my points here? Well there are many. Let's dig in a little bit deeper.

A lot of times we have been derailed off of the success track because of other people who have stopped and stalled our VIP timetable.

Yes we all have to work, and we all have objectives to take care of. We must of course make time for our obligations, agendas, and responsibilities. However, I'm here to tell you as your tough love coach that we must reclaim the power of our time. We must draw the line in the sand and say no to energy vampires, and people who waste our time. This will help you gain more time to help you work on your goals while protecting your mental, emotional, spiritual, and physical well-being.

Set yourself up for success by designating one day of the week, preferably Sunday, to plan out your entire rest of your week ahead. This will give you clarity on how you're going to spend your time, and make sure that you are using it wisely to get as much done without stress and with ease.

ENERGY VAMPIRES

Yes they are out there lurking, waiting to pounce on you and drain you of all of your energy, sucking the life right out of you. You must again be ready to get out of this sabotaging situation by reclaiming your time. Whether it's an old toxic friend that keeps pulling you into the drama, you must stay above the fray. Whether it's a toxic family member that wants to stir up drama, don't get tangled into their web. Use your time wisely and being productive and you'll have more traction in achieving your goals. We will talk more about this in November's chapter on how to create healthy boundaries.

PATIENCE: In Gods Time

> *"Patience is not the ability to wait, but the ability to keep a good attitude while waiting"*
> *-Jennifer Nicole Lee*

In one of my first books entitled: 'Crack Your Code: Unlock Your Fat Burning & Weight Loss Potential" I write about a certain condition that many of us suffer from. It is called "I-Want-It-Now-Itus". We all want to microwave success. We all want success to happen overnight. We have been raised in an environment of entitlement. We all want our results, and we wanted them yesterday! This is where we sabotage ourselves. We must learn to have patience.

A VIP woman is patient, able to wait, and she remains in an attitude of gratitude.

When someone is impatient, it evokes a sense of discord, uneasiness, and therefore stress. Patience attracts happiness, calmness, and a sense of being centered, balanced and grounded. When you are patient, you're also able to bring near to your heart which may be far in the future, while allowing something even better to fall in your original dreams place.

Yes I know, it sounds easier said than done. So here's my top list on how you can cultivate and grow your patience and have the patience of Job!

Let's get down to the "Zen of it"!

Zen Habits That Will Increase Your Patience:

1. What Triggers You: when you truly become aware of how and when you lose your patience, you understand the things that trigger you to go into that emotional dark hole. Is it when your family member does something in particular that is irritating? Is it when your children don't clean up after themselves? Is it when you have been working on a goal and you seem to be like a gerbil on a wheel going nowhere fast? Make a list of the ones that are more frequent. This is where your focus should be. And then eradicate the triggers. Or find a solution to the problem. Talk with your family member, let them know that what they're doing is irritating you. Or distance yourself from them. Have a good talk with your children and let them know that is essential for them to clean up after themselves.

And maybe with your goals, you've been doing the same thing over and over again, and expecting different results. Change your strategy but not your goals. This is where a good one on one private coaching session could come into play.

2. Count backwards from 5 to 1. I learned this technique when my children were small. They're innocent little toddlers, but sometimes as a mother you can lose your patience. When I found myself getting frustrated or angry, I stopped and we count slowly 5, 4, 3, 2, 1. When I was done the initial impulse to lose my cool, and do something rash out of frustration, went away. It helped me to be a better mother, and control my emotions. You can use this counting technique in any situation in your life where you feel you are losing your patience.

3. Mentally walk away. Taking a break from the situation that is triggering you to lose your patience, is also a Zen habit. Take the time out and take a break from the situation for 5 to 10 minutes. Let yourself calm down, and then strategically plan out your actions, write down your words of choice, and create a solution. Awaken your inner monk! And don't lose your cool!

4. Redirect your focus. If you're losing weight, or want a certain accomplishment to happen quicker, stop looking at the end result such as the number

on the scale, or finally accomplishing your goal. Instead shift your focus to the positive behaviors, habits, and the journey, and not the destination. If you're watching the pot waiting for it to boil, you can definitely lose your patience. This is a powerful metaphor telling you to stop looking at the results, and focus rather on the fabulous ride to your destination. Once I shifted my focus from wanting to lose weight, to working out and eating lean clean and green to be healthy, for energy stamina endurance, my results actually came that much quicker! So use the power of shifting your focus to what is actually important.

5.   Remember that things can take time. In this age of technology, we want things to happen fast and quick. So we must remind ourselves that good things can take time. If you expect things just to happen, and pop out of the hat like magic, you'll get impatient every time.

FUN WORK FOR JUNE:

How will you increase your joy:

_____

_____

_____

_____

_____

_____

_____

How will you make sure every day feels like a celebration, like your birthday?

_____

_____

_____

_____

_____

_____

_____

How do you plan on increasing your patience, so you will have more energy to be productive on your other goals and other areas of your life while you're waiting for other accomplishments to come to fruition?

_____

_____

_____

_____

_____

_____

_____

_____

_____

_____

_____

_____

_____

_____

NOTES FOR CHAPTER 6:

CHAPTER 7

JULY CELEBRATE YOUR WELLNESS FREEDOM! YOU ARE FREE TO BE A VIP!

Independence from Negativity, Toxic People, Lack, Suffering & Pain

Today we end all self-sabotage! Let us celebrate your Wellness Freedom! Let us be independent from all things that no longer serve us!-JNL

For anyone who left a horrible job, or finally was able to celebrate having a divorce finalized, or leaving a bad abusive relationship, or even getting rid of a toxic friend, you can understand first hand the importance of celebrating your independence, and freedom from being in that horrible relationship or situation. This is the same thing with your VIP power! Once you have reclaimed and unleashed your VIP power, looking at your life before you realized your VIP power, you could see that you actually were enchained, enslaved, and were held hostage by negative emotions, toxic environments, pessimistic people, buzzkills, energy vampires and other negative influences that have been obstructive to your enthusiasm and success in life. No longer do you have to deal with those fake friends who are uninterested and unresponsive to your success. No more adverse situations that are going to be damaging and detrimental to your future. Say "so long" to the unfavorable people, places, things, thoughts and habits that no longer serve your greater good. Since you have reclaimed and unleashed your VIP power, and you are surrounding yourself with positive people, employing an optimistic mind shift that allows you to be are constructive, and have endless enthusiastic energy. Enthusiasm is easy to come by when the conditions in your life are favorable. This leads me to the topic of freedom! Many think of living a healthy lifestyle that consists of exercising on a consistent level, along with eating healthy as boring and bland. They see it as a headache, or mind-numbing task that actually enclose you into a mental prison. For many coaching consultations, I was shocked to see that many had not made the VIP shift in mindset from seeing working out as a benefit instead of a disadvantage. Many look at working out as a job, homework, a chore, a dead-end responsibility, a problem or a burden.

But I'm here to dispel this myth and crush those lies. On the contrary, when you live a disciplined lifestyle, it unlocks your freedom.

This might sound like an oxymoron or that it contradicts itself. But, the more disciplined life you live, the more freedom you enjoy. How is this? This is because when you have a disciplined lifestyle, and you set boundaries for yourself, and you stick to the activities, actions, and daily habits that are in alignment with your dreams and goals, you no longer create havoc, headache, chaos, and confusion in your life. When you wake up at the same time every day, bright-eyed and bushy-tailed, with an attitude of gratitude, with your goals in front of you, and you know exactly what you are going to do, you are more in control, and yes, you have more freedom. You're not a slave to guessing. You take all the guesswork out of your day, which frees up your mental space so you are able to have laser-like focus and be more effective and efficient and yes with an upbeat attitude because again you are free to be a VIP!

To illustrate this point on how living a disciplined lifestyle can lead to freedom, and a liberated mental state, where you're able to concentrate and not be confused, I like to share a story with you of you when I became a mother. When I became a mother I got much unwanted advice from everybody including close family members and complete strangers. I could have listened to everybody and everyone, but I knew in my gut I had to find my own system that worked for me.

I found freedom in a very clear and concise schedule for my sons. This took out all the guesswork. When they were little I woke them up at the same time, bathed them at the same time, fed them at the same time, and had a very fabulous lineup of back-to-back events for them during the day. These events consisted of the basic necessities of eating, bathing time, play time, and intellectual stimulation. I knew exactly what I was doing at every minute of the hour. Why did I choose this method of raising my sons? Well, first my childhood all I remember is that my mother was frazzled, worried, riddled with anxiety, and really didn't even know what day of the week it was, and was very disorganized. Nothing against her, I'll remember it was very confusing for me and I felt unsafe, with little to no confidence, and that floated over into me having anxiety, stress, and worrying every day of what was going to happen.

So I flipped it. Instead of being frazzled, I became hyper-focused. Instead of going with the flow, I created my dream day. Instead of me having my head in the clouds and just believing that things happen for a reason, I made things happen. When I had my sons on a clear and organized schedule, if they were crying I would be able to decipher why they were crying. If they were crying and I just fed them, I knew that they were not hungry. Maybe it was gas. If they were crying but had not eaten in a while, I knew that they were hungry. If they were crying but I had just changed their diaper, I knew it wasn't because their diaper was dirty. Maybe they were in pain from something else. When I saw them getting tired, after their invigorating and stimulating educational playtime, I knew that I was able to entertain them just that much so they could be put down for a nice nap. I also made sure not to let them get overtired because when they would get overtired they would fight sleep and be cranky and not be able to calm down and get a good rest. So, my point here is: having a system and structure to your schedule will help you to be effective plus efficient, which results in being less stressed and more in control.

I was a happier mother which in turn made happier and more well-adjusted, bright, smart, and independent children who are also disciplined in their studies, and in their everyday life to-do's.

Now, I'm not here to preach about the way you should raise your children. However I'd like to use this drastic comparison of how my mother raised me, and how I decided to raise my son's because it took out all of the guesswork, all the mental stress, and the anxiety that would come with not having a disciplined lifestyle. To me, that's not a true reflection of freedom. Going with the flow is not freedom. Putting my VIP power into a disorganized, unstructured, and undisciplined daily lifestyle is like putting your beautiful diamonds in the dirty sewer. It makes no sense.

So, my goals in this chapter are for you to start associating living a disciplined, structured, and punctual lifestyle with clear intentions to equal freedom from fear, independence, chaos, and truly becoming liberated from being a complete hot mess!

Fall in Love with Structure: Congrats on starting a new love affair with living a structured lifestyle. This is a lifestyle that actually loves you back. Have you ever had that bad boyfriend? You know the one that was not good for you, but you kept on going back to over and over again after he would break your heart? It's kind of like doing a bad thing over and over again, because you're actually secretly addicted to the same outcome of the drama. We must break up with the bad boyfriend of being lazy, and not having a structured lifestyle, and finally marry Mr. Right, Mr. Right all the time, Mr. Discipline!

Marry Productivity As you have now broken up with Mr. Disorder, which only gave us a life of chaos, agitation, ignorance, confusion, negligence, and neglect, we're now ready to marry Mr. Discipline! What a great union! You will have more control and you will be more prepared. You will showcase more self-restraint. You will be able to develop healthier habits that stick. You will enjoy having an increased sense of balance, well-being, and being grounded.

Watch Out for the Success Traps: Sometimes it's that one friend who might seem to have your best interest at heart, but sadly enough she's the one that sabotages you with the invitations of the social events that derail your focus from your goals. Or maybe it is your coworker who wants to support you, but unintentionally distracts you from tasks at hand. So please watch out for the success traps. Maybe it's you associating being successful with having a few glasses of wine after every accomplishment, when it actually sets you back, as you may need to recover from a hangover, and or overeating due to the alcohol opening up your appetite. Watch out for these sneaky success traps that will disrupt your energy flow.

Override Your Biology: We as humans have been wired to do everything in our power to avoid pain. No wonder we don't like living a disciplined lifestyle. We have been brainwashed from birth that living a disciplined lifestyle is boring, hard, and for losers. But I'm here to dispel all those myths! On the contrary, living a disciplined lifestyle is one of joy, ease, and of inner peace knowing that you are doing all within your power to create a successful lifestyle. So, let's now retrain our brain to link pleasure to living a disciplined lifestyle, and pain to living a lifestyle of chaos and clarity.

Don't Be Tempted by Short-term Pleasures We live in a society where instant gratification is awarded. We are always seeking out quick avenues to happiness, short-term pleasures, and what can make us smile right here right now. This is where the power of visualization comes in. When you're living a disciplined lifestyle, keep the goal and end result in front of your mind's third eye. This will help you not to be tempted by short-term pleasure's which only detours you from the highway of success.

QUESTION: "Coach JNL, how can I learn to discipline myself?"

If your goal is to increase discipline in your life, you must take control of your habits and choices. Below are some powerful things you can do to master self-discipline, thus increasing your personal freedom.

- Know your weaknesses and flip them into strength by working on them every day.

- Remove temptations, so you will not unintentionally trigger yourself into self-sabotage.

- Set clear goals and have an execution plan.

- Trick yourself into being more disciplined by retraining your brain and your associations. Link pleasure to taking positive action, and link pain into not taking positive action.

- Streamline your activities by keeping it simple-streamline and take out all the unnecessary steps to meet your objective. For instance, if your goal is to lose weight, set up a training area in your home, which we call your VIP room, so you remove all those additional steps of getting to your car, driving to the gym, parking your car, walking up into the gym, going to the lockers to put your gym bag away. You get the point.

DECLARE YOUR FREEDOM FROM, WELL, UM, B.S.!

In closing this chapter, let us recite our Declaration of Freedom

I am free to be me!

I am free to be a VIP!

I am free to believe in me!

I am free from lack and suffering.

I'm free from other people's opinion.

I'm free from the pain of the past.

I am free from the mental enslavement of self-doubt, lack of confidence, and not believing in myself.

I am free from the past, as the past is not equal to the future.

I am free to dream as big as I want.

I am free to be unapologetically me!

I am free to enjoy my life.

I am free to create my own joy.

I am free from other people's opinions about me.

I am free to live a super healthy lifestyle, even if other people judge me and make unwanted comments.

I am free to love myself, just the way I am, right here right now as I work I'm continuing to better myself.

I am free of having to explain myself to others who do not believe in me, and who only to judge me.

And I am free to make the rest of my life the best of my life! I know the best is yet to come.

FUN WORK FOR CHAPTER 7:

Write below your action steps on how you plan on becoming more disciplined:

_____

_____

_____

_____

_____

_____

_____

_____

_____

NOTES FOR CHAPTER 7:

_____

_____

_____

_____

_____

_____

_____

_____

_____

_____

_____

_____

_____

_____

_____

_____

_____

_____

CHAPTER 8

AUGUST: AWESTRUCK, AWESOME A-HA AUGUST BACK TO YOU, BACK TO BASICS, MASTERING THE FUN-DAMENTALS TO SUCCESS

"Live in a never-ending state of awe of your miraculous life!"-JNL

August! This month is going to be a lot of fun! As we are working off of the theme of being "In Awe" and enjoying "A-ha Moments"!

To be "in awe" means to be in an overwhelming feeling of reverence, admiration, produced by something which is grand, sublime, and extremely powerful beyond measure! And that's the VIP life! One of constant celebration, one big party to be enjoyed and remembered and talked about for years to come.

So my intentions for you all in this chapter are to create everyday occurrences in your beautiful VIP lifestyle that make you live in awe, and in wonderment of the incredible beautiful life and miracles you enjoy daily!

A VIP woman always lives in awe. She's always in awe of her Higher Power. She is amazed of her own capabilities, and the everyday miracles that present themselves in her beautiful life. She lives in all of the everyday wonderment that's right before her. She's enlightened. She has experienced an awakening, and she never gives up and she never gives in! She knows how good it feels to get her workouts in and set her goals, she is the true architect of her own VIP life. She is creating moments of self-accomplishments that she will always look back upon and say "I DID THAT!" Her great sense of believing, and empowered faith, make her live in a continuous state of awesomeness!

She is a construction worker, building her dream life, one brick, one memory at a time. Sprinkling her future calendar with VIP powered events such as workouts, and creating unforgettable memories that will leave her in awe for years to come.

So, this month of August, we are going to focus on how to create more moments that make you live in awe, that are awesome! Remember, a VIP woman knows that she is co-creating her dream life with the universe. This is where the real miracles happen!

The VIP Woman knows that making VIP Moments is an art form!

I like to study happiness, looking into what creates long lasting happiness, and also wonderful memories to look back at that evoke a wonderful sense of well-being and joy.

If you are able to look back into your past and see an awe inspiring, awesome unforgettable life, while also having the energy, determination, and laser like focus to create more unforgettable memories in the future; then you have cracked the VIP code! As your coach, I'm going to give you the secret recipe on how to create a never-ending string of back-to-back VIP memories that will leave you in awe!

What are some of your Biggest A-Ha moments?

Take the time to look back and reflect on some of the biggest a-ha moments where you gained clarity in a nanosecond. It's as if an entire string of memories all added up to the exact moment where you had a breakthrough and had clarity on a certain specific topic in your life, and you had an awesome moment of enlightenment. I'll never forget my own personal "A-ha" moments.Take the time to write below your specific A-ha moments and how they shifted the direction of your life and made you realize what was important.

_____

_____

_____

_____

Why Was this A-Ha Moment so Profound for You?

_____

_____

_____

_____

_____

_____

_____

_____

What Clarity or Empowering Lesson did this A-Ha Moment Teach You?

_____

_____

_____

_____

_____

_____

_____

What Pivotal Direction Did This A-Ha Moment Guide You To Take?

_____

_____

_____

_____

_____

_____

_____

_____

Let's create more of these powerful VIP memories and moments that will continue to shape our VIP lives!

We are Memory Architects.

We can influence what we remember, and also what we create in the future.

Do you ever feel like past memories have been so traumatic to you, hurtful, that they actually negatively impact your future? I know this has been the case for many of my VIP clients. We sadly enough are being forced to create our past over and over again. We must release these negative emotions linked to these past hurtful memories. In this powerful VIP exercise we are going to erase these memories from our subconsciousness, never to allow them to taint our future again. We are going to use the powerful technique of visualizations to free ourselves mentally of any past negative emotions that have flowed over into our present current state, which then in turn impact our future decisions and outcomes.

SCRATCH OVER IT In this powerful exercise I want you to take the memories that have crippled you in the past and currently show up in your future. The goal and intention of this "scratch over it" exercise is for you to actually take a razor blade, a sharp pain, a needle, and scratch back and forth over the memory as if you were taking even a knife over an old photograph scratching the memory out from your past. As you mentally are scratching back and forth with your object of choice, see the memory disappearing into nothingness. You're going to see the white background of the photograph appearing as you keep on scratching back and forth. Now you've totally scratched over it, as if it never happened. You are free from being enslaved to these past negative memories.

RIP IT UP Take the negative memory that you want to get rid of, the one that you find recurring time and time again in your current and future state, and rip it up. Imagine you're opening up a book, or even a magazine, and you see that negative experience. I want you to rip it out of the book or magazine. Then rip it into a hundred pieces, then put it in the garbage to never be seen again. It no longer has control over you and you are free from this negative memory wiping your slate clean with every rip.

BURN IT One very impactful coaching exercise that I've done with my VIP clients is that I actually had them write down all of their negative experiences, or the people that hurt them, and then write a letter of empowerment. In this letter, you are to write your feelings, and not hold back. Let it all out. You might cry. You might scream. But it is important that you relive this memory and don't suppress it. If you suppress it it'll only cause damage to your spirit. Our objective is healing. You must heal yourself 1000% and not leave anything unsaid or unfelt. Now, once you have written all of your emotions, all of your feelings, and even directed this letter to someone in specific that hurt your feelings, I want you to also forgive them. Now, just because you forgive them does not mean that you are allowing them to do that to you in the future. As the famous quote goes, "holding onto anger is like grasping a hot coal with the intent of throwing it at someone else. You are the only one that gets burned." It is written in the Bible, in Colossians Chapter 3 verse 13, it states "forgive as the Lord forgave you." So aim to forgive so you may release all of the blessings that are in store for you, and heal yourself from the hurtful past.

So, now that you have your letter, you are going to have a burning ceremony. Remember, safety first. Make sure you have a large metal bowl or even over your kitchen sink with water nearby. I usually have my VIP clients do it in their kitchen sink so it is near the water and it is safer. As you read this letter out loud, forgive yourself for allowing yourself to hold onto anger and resentment for so long. You are now releasing it. You were going to light a flame underneath this letter and watch it burn. Allow it to burn completely turning it to black ash. Then rinse it down the sink. Say a silent prayer of gratitude knowing that you are now moving onwards and up allowing the negative past to be completely forgotten and forgiven.

Now that we have cleaned up any negative past experiences by any and all of the above VIP techniques, you are now ready to create new powerful memories that will empower you, satisfy your spirit, and feed your emotions the positive vibrations that you are worthy and deserving of experiencing daily.

FLUSH IT:

Out of all the techniques, this is probably one of my favorites. It proved to be very powerful for me and many past situations. It is such a powerful metaphor. Think about it. Not to get too detailed here, but when you use the ladies room, you just flush it. Out of sight and out of mind, you simply move on. Same thing with bad experiences. If someone attacks your dignity, if someone disrespects you, if you find yourself reliving an embarrassing moment over and over again- Just flush it!

I often joke with my coaching clients that there's a big toilet out in outer space, I call it the "Cosmic Commode". What a visual! Where you empty all of your negative memory bank every night before you go to bed. A huge white floating commode just drifting in the Galaxy!

So, if you ever have a negative memory pop up, take it straight to the "Cosmic Commode" and flush it! Bid it farewell as you hold down the handle, and believe you me there's some days where I just keep that handle down and keep it on a constant flush! So, next time you find yourself having a Civil War in your mind over past experiences that have nothing to do with your future well-being, make it straight to the big commode and outer space and give it a good flush!

Plan Your Successes in Advance: Put Them Into Your Calendar

Right now take out your calendar. Let's look at your calendar until the end of the year. Then even look into the next year. It is time to do some fun work. Every month I want you to plan a VIP experience. It could be something so simple as watching all of your favorite movies, or taking a fun stay-cation in your local town, or planning an event at your home with special VIP friends that you know will always bring the positive vibes. This is important because now you have an anchor, a magnet pulling you into the future to create your VIP dream life. You can plan anything you wish, your heart's desire.

Maybe it's one day a month where you do a spa day, or you can enjoy signing up for a cooking class. You can reconnect with an old friend and have a fun "Girlfriends" day out. You can meet up with a fellow VIP that you never met and make it a fun VIP day of window shopping, having a healthy lean, clean and green lunch, or even doing a master goal setting session.

VIP IT UP! By now we all can see that living the VIP life is a nonstop party! And even though the word VIP stands for "very important person", it is taking on a larger meaning. When I hear the word VIP, I think of these adjectives:

- Special

- Elite

- Royal

- One of a kind

- Special privileges

- Upper class status

- Increased importance

So, let's take one of these adjectives one by one, and create special memories that will evoke these feelings and themes.

How can you make your life more special? How can you make your future memories more special?

_____

_____

_____

_____

_____

_____

How can you dissect yourself from the pact and make your energy more elite, where people actually seek you out to spend time with you or even just talk with you? Maybe it's your VIP way of looking at life? The Paradigm that you live life through. Always looking at life with rose colored glasses on, or actually VIP glasses on!

_____

_____

_____

_____

_____

_____

How can you project your energy to be more royal?

_____

_____

_____

_____

_____

_____

_____

_____

How can you create more "one-of-a-kind" experiences?

_____

_____

_____

_____

_____

_____

_____

_____

How can you create more future memories that give you more special privileges?

_____

_____

_____

_____

_____

_____

_____

How can you create more future memories that give you that sense of "upper class status"?

_____

_____

_____

_____

_____

_____

_____

What future events and activities can you create that will give you an increased sense of importance?

_____

_____

_____

_____

_____

_____

_____

_____

QUESTION: "Dear Coach, JNL: How can I live an exciting 'Red Carpet' Life without sabotaging all of my focus with eating healthy and working out. If I eat lean, clean and green, and train like an athlete at www.JNLVIP.com but then I'm invited to parties, where I know there's going to be unhealthy food, tempting dishes that are high in calories, and tons of alcoholic beverages, How can I still live the exciting VIP life without sacrifice?"

ANSWER: Great question! I would like to use one of my beautiful VIPs who lives in Great Britain by the name of Natasha as an example. She was doing great on her VIP program. She was eating so healthy, and getting her workouts in too. She got dressed up one evening, looking ever so beautiful, and she knew what was ahead of her; endless servings of unhealthy food, sweets and desserts, and sugary alcoholic beverages that are full of empty calories. So, what she did was ask the hostess if she could bring a salad. Problem solved! Instead of feeling forced to eat the unhealthy options, she brought a healthy choice, therefore motivating the other partygoers to enjoy healthier options as well.

Dull and Mundane, or Over the Top-It's Your Life, Its Your Choice!

We have been brainwashed by society that if you were born into a certain social class or economic status in life, that you are stuck there. But this is where your VIP power is born, evoked, and strengthened. Many of you know my story. I was born to first-generation Italian immigrant parents. I was raised on food stamps. I was teased and bullied for my dark olive colored skin in a very small rural southern town. But I always knew I was destined to do great things. That was the seed to my VIP power. I didn't listen to the bullying, and teasing. I actually let it strengthen me.

Fast forward to today, I teach in my online coaching program and to all my clients around the world that you have a choice daily. To live the dull and mundane life or you can create one that is over-the-top fabulous. Whatever you love to do, do it, and do it for you. Whether it's putting on your favorite workout gear for your VIP exercise sweat sessions, or getting dressed up for a night out on the town, or going to the symphony, or even doing an at-home spa night, you must enjoy the VIP life! Sprinkle your calendar with events that will make you smile. Salt and pepper your weekly schedule with VIP experiences that will warm your spirit. And no, you don't need to spend a lot of money to feel like the VIP that you are. So go for it!

Emotional Highlighter Pen Now as you are truly stepping into your VIP power, reclaiming it, and unleashing it, we're going to take it a step further. Imagine your life as a book. Break out your neon yellow highlighter and use it as an emotional highlighter pen to showcase the most memorable moments in your life. Let's make this into a powerful meditation. Right now think of the top unforgettable moments that have made you transition into becoming the best version of yourself. Think about all of those "A-ha moments" where you were at a crossroads, and you finally took drastic and immediate action to change your life. Or think about the time you truly felt beautiful. Think about the time you looked in the mirror and actually fully loved everything about yourself. Maybe it was the time you left a hurtful relationship. Maybe it was the time you left a job where you didn't feel appreciated. Maybe it was when you danced all night until your feet hurt or you actually broke the heel off of your shoe. Maybe it was when you laughed so hard that you got cramps in your stomach. Maybe it was when you crushed your goals and you experienced that fabulous feeling of victory.

Now, take all of this positive energy, and take your virtual neon yellow highlighter and highlight those experiences in your life. Pull them to the forefront of your memory. Put them in the top part of your memory bank right at the top of your brain. Whenever you're feeling challenged, look back at the beautiful memories of your life, where you used your emotional highlighting pen to bring attention to these amazing memories. This will give you the strength, and the VIP power to carry on and unleash your power on another level.

Harness the Power of Firsts-

Do you want to know one of the top VIP success keys to creating more memories that will make you happy? Simply create more "first" memories. Think about it, have you ever noticed how when you were a child all the way up until 30, life went very slow? I mean as a child seemed like it took forever for Christmas to come! And then after you hit the age of 30, it's as if life speed up tremendously. Why? It's called the reminiscent effect. One theory is that this reminiscent era is more memorable because our teens and early adult years are our defining years or our formative years. Think about it look at the list of memories below, I know you can remember all of these very distinctly. It's almost as if you took an emotional highlighter pen to these memories and you can conjure them up very quickly.

First job

First kiss

First pet

First day of school

When your child is took his or her first steps

Your first time traveling by yourself

Your first time driving your car.

Your first date.

Your first vacation

Your first time eating certain foods

You get the point!

So how do we take this information in and make it work to our advantage to increase happier memories?

We create more firsts!

This is why I'm always switching up the workouts. Also this is the exact reason why I'm always trying new and different foods. To keep it exciting, fun, and fresh! The first time fitting into a certain dress size in a while. Or the first time you were able to zip up your pants and button them after a few years. first time completing five workouts in one week. The first time eating lean clean and green for the entire month. See this is the new exciting way to live life and to create happier memories by making more "first" experiences.

FUN WORK:

Right now, take out your calendar, and look at the next few months, straight into the new year. Strategically plan "firsts" into your future. This will not only be exciting for you, but you've already built in magnets into your future, helping you to wake up with more passion, purpose, excitement, and clear distinct vision for your future! Feel the excitement as you are planning some new, fresh, and positive experiences that will add tons of happiness and joy to your life and your future memory bank.

Write some things below that you would like to relive again as "firsts".

Possibly your first kiss with your true love-why not "script it out" and re-live it again!

Driving your dream car for the first time. Next time you go into your car, grip the steering wheel with excitement and joy as if it was your first time driving your car. Feel that youthful Joy surge through every cell of your body. Basically, this luxury for granted, because remember how new and exciting it was to experience your freedom for the first time?

Moving into your dream home. You may not be in your dream home, but that should not stop you from entering into your home, that is yours, that is filled with love, light and laughter! Pretend you are moving into your dream home and you open up the door for the first time and your eyes are seeing your dream home. Feel the excitement! Remember when you manifest you must feel it not just think it.

Finally landing or creating your dream job. Remember when you finally landed that dream job, or your first job. How excited were you? Don't let that excitement ever leave you. Conjured up again and let's create new firsts today!

NOTES:

_____

_____

_____

_____

_____

_____

_____

Your A-Ha Moments That Have Shaped and Defined You!

First of all I'd love to explain what an "A-ha" moment is. An "A-ha" moment is when you become enlightened, it's almost as if an internal light bulb goes off in your brain, shining light on what you so consciously already knew, but it has become more apparent impressionable in your life more than ever.

It could be a moment of instant insight, a flash of sudden inspiration, or in a split-second you are able to comprehend a vast amount of information. You could even see a fast forward flash into the future, or you can see yourself from the outside looking in. Or it could be you just becoming more self-aware of how your decisions are impacting your future.

We have all had these moments, these defining A-Ha moments of clarity, where we become awoken, and enlightened beyond words. These "A-Ha" moments are almost like a spiritual awakening, where in a split-second, you have eternal insight, your third eye is able to see the larger bigger picture.

Let me share with you some of my own personal "A-Ha" moments

1. When I was little I would see my mother always complain that she never had enough money, and she would blame it on my dad, her ex-husband.

She would say if it wasn't for your father we wouldn't be living like this. Even though I was little, I had an "A-ha" moment from listening to my mother speak. Right then and there, even though I was under the age of 10, I made a conscious decision to never be financially dependent on another person, especially a man, not even my husband.

2.   I remember when I would "yo-yo diet". The last time I "yo-yo" dieted I completely killed my metabolism. It was in 1997 and I had just finished college. I knew I wanted to get under a hundred and twenty pounds. It seemed like a pretty fancy number. My goal was 117 pounds and it sounded good to me. Even though I'm close to 5'9, being under a hundred and twenty pounds was a goal of mine. Looking back, it didn't make any sense. However I'm glad I went through this experience to become stronger and truly understand what being healthy meant. So, I became the "Cardio Queen". I would do two hours a day of cardio. I would do one hour of cardio on the bike, the one hour of cardio on elliptical. Mind-numbing cardio. I would not go near any weights because I was afraid of getting bulky and big, and also gaining weight. I also cut calories to under a thousand calories a day. No whole fruits or vegetables, only a small bowl of pasta, I don't know why I chose that. I figured it was fat free

and the carbs were okay. Fast forward to the end result; I got under a hundred twenty pounds, actually 118 pounds to be exact. When I looked at the scale, I was happy for a split second, and then reality sunk in. I realized that I had locked myself into a corner. How can I continue doing 2 hours of cardio day? How can I continue eating only a thousand calories a day, with no fat in my diet. This was absolutely Hell On Earth! It was as if I put handcuffs on myself, and chained myself to my diet and obsessive working out, only doing cardio. I didn't get fit. I actually got sick. I remember being so exhausted I could not even walk up the stairs. I wanted to lay in bed all day, because I killed my metabolism, and I was suffering from metabolic damage. My hair was thinning out, I had no get up and go, and my feet felt like cement blocks. And yes, I was a "skinny fat" person. The number on the scale might have been pretty, but when I looked in the mirror I was flabby everywhere. With little to no energy. Then it only got worse. Since I killed my metabolism, whatever I ate stayed on my body. I gained so much weight so fast that I ballooned up to 180 lb. At that time I said forget it. So I ate, ate and ate some more. And that's when I met my husband. I was at 180 lbs. I got pregnant and we sadly suffered a miscarriage. Then I got pregnant with Jaden, then I got pregnant with Dylan. So, for 5 years I was just either pregnant, breastfeeding, or just straight-up out of shape. So, I had totally hit rock bottom, that led me to my next "A-ha" moment.

In this A-ha moment, I realized that being a certain number on the scale did not mean being healthy. I knew that I could not be healthy by just doing cardio, or just by eating carbs with no fat. I knew that I had to get strong. I was so tired of being weak and exhausted. I wanted to feel empowered, strong, almost like a superhero that jumped right out of the comics. Like Wonder Woman, like Superwoman, a woman with muscles. That's when I started looking at the fitness magazines of women that had more of a muscular physique, and that healthy vibrant glow of energy. In 2003, I had asked my husband to take a photo of me which would now become my infamous before photo. I put on the only bikini I had, a hot pink fuchsia two-piece, I through my hair into a bun, and my husband took photos of me with our Polaroid camera; yes, the one that actually gave you a little small square of a photo that you had to flip very fast for it to develop. I just gave birth to my second son Dylan who was three months old at the time. I knew I was out of shape. But, I had one of the biggest "A-Ha" moments that catapulted me, scared me, and forced me to quantum leap and take immense drastic action into getting healthy. Right then and there when I looked back at the photo, I was completely shocked. I saw an unhealthy, unkept, frazzled, exhausted woman who suffered from chronic fatigue.

Remember, I had miscarried before Jaden. Then 3 months later I got pregnant with Jaden. After Jaden, I became pregnant again with Dylan. This photo was actually taken when Dylan was about three months old. It was such a scary photo to look at, I didn't even recognize who this person was. This "A-ha" moment was a deciding moment, where I was at the crossroads of life where I could either continue to be unhealthy and follow in the footsteps of my mother, and her mother, and the entire lineage of women who emotionally ate, and let themselves go. Or, I could take serious positive action to start living my healthiest best life. Looking back, I'm so grateful that I took that before photo. That was one of the most powerful "A-ha" moments of my life.

FUN WORK: Write below some of your most powerful "A-ha" moments. Where were you? What was going on? How did those moments shift you, and redirect you to become better and stronger?

_____

_____

_____

_____

_____

_____

_____

_____

_____

_____

_____

_____

_____

_____

_____

_____

_____

Let's kick it up a notch. We are going to weave into our future some redefining "A-ha" moments that celebrate your VIP power.

Use your Mirror Neurons:

When you're invited to go to a party, be in awe of yourself as you're getting dressed and ready to go. Tell yourself how fabulous, beautiful, and gorgeous you are. When you enter the room, visualize that you have your VIP power and keep on flowing off your back, with your chest up, shoulders back, abs pulled in, chest, back and glutes lifted. As you walk, walk with confidence not cockiness. Take notice of other people's faces and how they are responding to your VIP energy. This is a new a-ha moment. Seeing how other people look at you with positive energy back. Remember mirror neurons always work. If you enter a room confident, people will be confident around you.

Back to You, Back to Basics

> *"Mastering the basics of any program is the key to lifelong success When you master yourself, and master the basics, you crack your success code"!-JNL*

Remember, every master once was a beginner. And here's another truth. Sadly enough 95% of us slide back into our old habits, back into a hermit crab shell, back to our outdated selves. So, instead of evolving, we de-evolve. Why? Exactly the topic I'm going to be covering here. The basics. Everyone wants to microwave success. Everyone wants to have instantaneous success overnight. A lot of people are like, "coach I want to have 10 years of success in two weeks". And they're looking at me like I have a magic wand. But it's you reading this now that has to do the inner work in order to enjoy the outer work. So, just as a karate instructor, or a drill sergeant, or a teacher will hammer into their students, you must master the basics.

What are the basics to the VIP lifestyle?

- Training consistently, 4-6 times per week.

- Waking up the same time and going to bed the same time every day, even on the weekends.

- Eating healthy all the time, with an occasional cheat bite here or there.

- Get your adequate rest

- Setting your boundaries.

- Respect your time by not wasting it.

- Remaining in an attitude of gratitude.

- Praising it up so that the miracles come down.

- Always looking at the brighter side of things.

- Never giving up.

- And yes being persistent, allowing yourself to grow strong every day, stacking the building blocks of success, one brick at a time.

Here's a quick little side story that will give you a very powerful visual of why it's important to learn the basics and hammer them into perfection over and over again.

My sons were in their teenage years, they became black belts at a very successful martial arts school here in Miami. Their instructor had them repeat over and over again the fundamental drills that a novice would have to do as if it was their first day. I often wonder why he would make them repeat things that they knew already. But I saw the magic in this brilliance. He wanted to instill in them persistence, endurance, stamina, discipline, and other characteristics needed in order to grow and get to a black belt and then stay there. At first they would say he was being a mean and cruel instructor. But on second hand when I took a closer look, he was building their persistence, the resilience, and the muscle memory that it needed to actually become a master at their art form in martial arts.

Now as your VIP master trainer and transformational Coach, let me take it up a notch.

If you are a beginner VIP, or an expert VIP member, always when you're learning a new skill begin with the attitude of expecting mastery. So if it's your goal to learn something new, you must start with the expectation that you are eventually going to become a master of it. No matter how long it'll take, you are starting this journey expecting to become an expert and a master of this skill. So always think of yourself as a top pro in training. You're going to learn how to do a glute bridge squeeze, think of yourself as a future professional "booty-builder" and a master at glute workouts. If you're learning new leadership skills, see yourself as a future world class level leader. If you're learning public speaking, begin with the expectation that you will eventually become one of the top speakers in the industry, even if it's going to take you decades to get there. When you make this shift mentally, you're going to transition your energy from "let me hurry up and get there and achieve this goal in two weeks", to "I am going to focus and work really work hard on the basics, and no matter how long it takes!" You see, you must make the decision to become a disciplined learner and to handle the basics nearly flawlessly.

Live in the moment: By mastering the basics, over and over again, it's going to give you the foundation that you need to live in the moment, giving you a happier life. If you're always looking at the end result, you're going to put yourself in an imaginary prison, and handcuff yourself to the end result.

Remember, there is no magic wand and you cannot microwave success. Yes, it might be painful, yes it might be grueling, yes it might be at times uncomfortable. Sadly enough, society has babied us and has made us expect things to be just given to us. But I am here to tell you that you must earn it.

If you want to have a strong body, you have to train it to be strong. If you want to eat like an athlete, you have to eat super clean and strategically. If you want to reshape, and transform your body to look like a VIP Queen who is chiseled out of stone, you're going to have to push past the point of pain on some training days which might be uncomfortable. So pick your hard.

So again, be committed to mastering the basics. One of the reasons many people fail to advance is that they don't build a solid enough foundation of the basics. They cripple and suffocated their progress by forcing themselves to move forward beyond skills that they haven't quite mastered yet. Like time management, and being consistent. You cannot get the results of five workouts per week by only doing two workouts. You must master time management, and delegating, and also the basics of getting up early and going to bed early. Think about it, if you cannot master basic arithmetic, you'll never progress to algebra. The same is true for fitness, success, and pretty much any field and industry. You must master the basics first, no matter how long it takes. As your coach, I'm here to help you earn an "A" and every single basic skill before you move on to the advanced skills. This is the fastest way to learn in the long run.

If you had a bad coach in the past and started a fad diet, you are not alone. We have all been there. But we can correct this past by not looking for the quick, fast and easy approach to being healthy. Lets take full responsibility now as an adult to correct it. Right now we are going to unlearn to relearn and become the VIP success stories that we deserve, by yes, mastering the basics!

VIP SUCCESS TIP: I also want to cover the subject of personal management as well. You can get every app, fancy technology, timers, buzzers, and put post-it notes everywhere to become better organized, but it won't mean anything if you haven't mastered the basic skill of self-discipline. Putting extra technology into a person who is not disciplined is not going to help. Master self-discipline first, and also declutter your life, getting rid of all things, habits, people and activities that bring you down, drain your energy, and leave you unfocused.

Mastering the "Fun-damentals" to Success

You are reading this right now because you are ready to take control of your life and create the lifestyle you want to live. You know that it is possible to create your dream life, and to continuously reclaim and unleash your VIP power. This means being consistent. This means mastering the basics. Again, we cannot microwave success and success doesn't happen overnight. As your transformational coach, it is my goal to help you become excellent in life and become the person you want to be.

However, it's going to take focus, dedication, building consistency, and being persistent, which equates to mastering the basics.

Life mastery is about becoming better each and every day, pushing yourself to the limits. Yes, some days will be better than others, but over time and when you continuously master the basics, you will achieve all of your dreams and goals. Below I have outlined some necessary steps you can take to master your life, and build upon your basics every day. Think about your success as a staircase to the top. Every basic fundamental behavior and daily skill you master, you are ready to go to take the next step up.

TAP INTO THE POWER OF POSITIVE THINKING:
Your mind is your strongest muscle. If you master the mind, you can master your entire life. Everything starts in the mind and then flows into the body. You must do the inner work in order to enjoy the outer work. Your mind is incredibly powerful and can quite literally create its own reality. Grab hold of this VIP power, and when you start every morning, go straight into an attitude of gratitude, and positive thinking. It sets the tone for the day. Remember, if you win the morning, you win the day. If you win the day you win the weeks. If you win the week you win the month. If you win the months you win the years. If you win the years you win at life. You can do what works for you. You can go through your positive "I

Am" affirmations, or list off everything you're grateful for.

For example, I tap into the power of positive thinking right in the morning by going through my tried-and-true affirmations which go something like this; "Thank you God for today! Thank you God for my strong healthy mind and body. Thank you for another opportunity to do good, to help others, and to be an amazing mom and wife. I'm grateful for this moment and I know that I'm going to create magic and miracles today. I'm feeling too blessed to be stressed and I'm ready to seize the day!" This gets you tuned into a vibration of being proactive, and creating the life that you deserve.

LIVE INTENTIONALLY AND DON'T REACT: Now that we've changed our mindset and attitude towards life, we're ready to take it to the next level. By not reacting, you are going to then be more proactive, and you are no longer going to react to your surroundings and your environment. Instead, you are going to live intentionally and live on purpose. What does proactive behavior look like? It is all about planning and taking action on your plans. You as a VIP woman now know that no one is going to be able to accomplish any of your goals for you except for you. If you want to get in shape, become financially independent, or land your dream job, it boils down to one person - you! So, live with intention, by always keeping your end goal in sight. Vision boards or even your vision journal are very powerful tools to help you live intentionally.

Don't exhaust yourself by reacting to outside stimuli that triggers you in a negative way. Get rid of all negative triggers, and replace them with positive ones. When you find yourself wanting to react, use my VIP 10-second behavior hack: when you feel triggered to react in a negative way, take a deep breath and count slowly backwards from ten all the way to one. This will stop you from reacting in a negative way that might make you feel guilty or ashamed afterwards. Get control of your emotions and don't let them control you. When you get to one, you're going to have more clarity on the situation. Ask yourself "what is the end result that I want here?" and "how can I take the higher road?" and "How can I respond, or not respond, so that I will be proud of myself?"

EAT, TRAIN, SLEEP, REPEAT: Have you ever seen the meme or the motivational quote that says "eat, train, sleep and repeat"? Well it's true! That's how you build consistency, and master the basics. If you want to lose weight, and also maintain your weight loss results, you've got to marry the notion and commit to understanding, you must eat like an athlete, train like an athlete, sleep like an athlete, and repeat. It's a cycle. You cannot expect to do a wellness program for two weeks and then be healthy for the rest of your life. That's why you must shift your focus away from the end result, the number on the scale, or certain dress size, and shift your focus to the beautiful journey, not just the destination.

PREPARE, SCHEDULE, PLAN: One of the biggest a-ha moments I've had on my own personal wellness journey and also as a transformational coach is the power of preparing, scheduling, and planning. These three powerful activities are the foundations of actually taking action. People do not take action because they failed to prepare, schedule, or plan. You must prepare yourself, for instance, to do your weekly workouts by circling on your calendar which ones you're going to do. Then prepare your workout clothes. Prepare your VIP workout area. Prepare your detox water, and schedule it on your calendar. If it's not put on your calendar, it's not going to happen. Put your workouts as important business meetings that you cannot be late to, call in sick to, or not show up to; after all, these meetings are with the most important person in the world - you! Then you must plan your entire life around these appointments. Yes it is true, these are the most important appointments on your calendar. That's why I go ahead and plan my entire month's workouts at the beginning of every month. For example, this is August, right before August is over about three weeks into the month, I will go ahead and do my schedule for September's workouts. Making sure I trained four to six times a week. Then I schedule all of my other appointments around my workouts. I also designate one day of the week for my grocery hauls, and meal preps. This will set me up for success for the entire week! Make this a habit that you master, and you will be enjoying this journey so much more. Take out the stress from the process and make it fun. When I prepare, schedule, or plan, I put on fun music, get my calendars out, and enjoy creating my dream life. I get so excited when I see all of the workouts on my calendar. I know that I'm creating such a healthy future for me and my loved ones. When I work out I'm happier and healthier, that means my family, clients, and loved ones are going to be happier and healthier too.

CONTINUOUSLY SET GOALS: Living life with no goals is like driving a boat without a rudder. You're going to be all over the place. So constantly set goals for yourself. For example I like to set monthly goals and annual goals. Long-term goals are the annual goals. Short-term goals are the monthly goals. As soon as you crush one goal, continuously set new goals. It's like climbing a mountain. Just because you climb one mountain doesn't mean you're not going to climb any more mountains! I mean, why stop? Get ready to have a continuous procession of goals that are going to be pulling you forward towards your successful life, One goal at a time. That's how you master the basics. I've always been moving forward. These future goals are like magnets drawing you forward, not allowing you to shrink back into your past.

When you set goals, you actually crush sneaky counter-intentions. When we don't have a goal in front of us, we find ourselves looking back to the past when we failed, or when that person hurt us, or when we tried and couldn't get the results that we wanted. So, by continuously setting goals you will be pushing yourself into the future or further away from your negative past. Keep yourself so busy that you do not have time to be down, sad, reflect on the negative memories, or fall into a trap of feeling sorry for yourself because of what somebody did to you 10 years ago. Continue to set goals and crush them!

FUN-WORK:

Use this space below to write down your action plan of how you are going to master the basics.

_____

_____

_____

_____

_____

_____

_____

_____

_____

NOTES FOR CHAPTER 8:

CHAPTER 9

SEPTEMBER: A SEPTEMBER TO REMEMBER! STRONG MIND, BODY, SPIRIT. MENTAL TOUGHNESS, EMOTIONAL STRENGTH, AND A BODY THAT IS STRONGER THAN EVER! FALL IN LOVE & FALL FORWARD IN FAITH

"Take the time to look back to see just how far you've come and all the success you have created! Fall in love with the new and improved you. Fall forward in faith! This will be a September to remember!

Welcome to September! The month where we celebrate the first day of fall. What a glorious time! Let us enjoy the transition where the leaves start turning the beautiful autumn colors representing another season of life. Moving forward from the strength and mastering the basics we learned from last month, we're going to continue and touch up on mental toughness, increasing our emotional strength, and building a body that is stronger than ever. We're going to learn how to fall in love again with ourselves, and fall forward in faith, and faith it until we make it.

Mental Toughness

You might be thinking "why is Coach JNL telling me about mental toughness? I just want to lose weight and be able to squeeze back into my bikini." Well this is exactly where mental toughness comes into play. We have to get out of the old, archaic, "dinosaur", outdated version of thinking in black and white, of calorie in and calorie out. If you don't have the mental toughness, or the mental resilience to be persistent, and learn how to tough it out during tough times; and rough it out during rough times, you'll never make it.

Mental toughness not only comes into play with wellness, fat loss, and gaining muscle mass, but it is beneficial in all areas of your life.

Don't you agree that 90% of the time life does not turn out as easy as you'd it like to, or as you had planned? So, when life sucker punches you, or kicks you in the stomach, we all just want to curl up with a big bowl of ice cream and hide under the covers, or drink your problems away, but this is where your mental toughness kicks in. When life is throwing you chaos from every direction, you have to have the mental toughness, and the discipline, to wake up, show up, dress up, never give up, and give yourself your very own motivational kick in the butt! You have to have the mental toughness to find the calmness in the chaos.

When you strengthen yourself mentally nothing, nobody, and no situation can knock you off your path of success. Take this instance for example.

One of my VIP clients finally decided to reclaim her VIP power. In the past year she had gained 60 pounds. She had become lethargic suffering from chronic fatigue just from the mere fact of not exercising and having poor nutritional habits. We did a coaching consultation. I flipped her VIP switch on. She started waking up early, doing her VIP workout first thing in the morning to supercharge their day. She started eating lean, clean and green, making sure to get her green smoothie in before she went to work and packing her lunch. She was on a really good success spiral, and was losing weight and feeling great. Well, her husband wasn't so happy about this. His insecurities kicked in, because he saw that she finally woke up and became aware of her VIP power. Well her new VIP Power obviously threatened him, and he pulled some sabotaging moves out of his big bag of tricks. He started shaming her for wanting to look good, even going to the extent of accusing her of cheating on him. He was telling her negative things like "who are you getting sexy for? What's your boyfriend's name? Let me see your phone? I want to see who you've been texting!" It got quite ugly. So she shut down. But, she didn't shut down for long. When many women would just crawl back into their hermit crab shell, and go back to suffering from chronic fatigue and being lethargic, she dusted off her VIP cape and turned up the VIP power even more.

You see, that's why mental toughness is so important. When she could have slipped all the way back down to where she started into a deep dark hole of depression and anxiety; allowing him to control her, she didn't! She kicked it into 6th gear!

I did a coaching consultation with her and I'm grateful that I equipped her with the VIP power that she needed to push through the pain. She finally realized that he was not healthy for her, very controlling, extremely demeaning, and condescending to her. That's why she sunk into this deep depression before and had allowed herself to lose herself which led to her and gaining 60 pounds.

Okay so now we understand the benefits of being mentally strong. How can you gain mental strength? Easily! The more you stick to your guns, and have strong decision-making muscles, and always choose what is in your best interest, you will start to see this healthy pattern of self-love and self-respect. Whenever you come to a crossroads in life, sometimes you have to make tough decisions. As I like to say sometimes, it is what it is. Sometimes it's not right, sometimes it's not wrong, but it's just the decision you have to make in order to set yourself up for success.

TOP HACKS TO HELP YOU GET MENTALLY TOUGH:

Push The Boulder Up the Mountain: Powerful Law of Contrast.

Every morning when you wake up, visualize something very hard that you have to do. I started doing this mind hack long ago when I found that I had a tremendous amount of work load every day and it really helps. In order to be successful, you've got to work, and work a lot. So, with this mind hack, not only did I flip the switch in my brain to see my enormous amount of workload as easy, I also made it fun as well. Right when I wake up, I tell myself that it's time to push the boulder up the mountain. My body actually feels the physical deep pressure of pushing a huge thousand pound rock boulder up a mountain. For a split second, I feel overwhelmed, but then I remind myself that it's only imaginary, and so it's kind of fun that it's not real. Keep following me. So, I take myself to an extreme mental, physical, and emotional visual that I would have to conjure up all my energy to do that is extremely difficult mentally and physically. Once I've accepted that I have to push the boulder up the mountain, everything else that I have to do that day is extremely easy and fun. This is such a powerful metaphor, it sounds a little bit silly, but boy does it work. After visualizing me physically pushing a 1000 pound rock boulder up a mountain and I look back at my work that I have to do for the day, it actually seems easier and fun.

Strengthen Your Decision Making Muscles: The VIP power of being able to have strong decision-making muscles will help you also become mentally tougher. In life, and sometimes under a time crunch, you have to make decisions. I have been fortunate enough to coach many women, and what I found is that the ones that are highly successful, and extremely prolific and powerful was that they're able to make decisions and THEN STICK WITH THEM! They might get backlash from their family, their friends might not like their decisions; but they make decisions based on what is best for them and also their immediate loved ones. And yes, they don't move backwards, they move forwards and stand by their decisions.

You see, when you stop the popularity contest, and stick to your guns, you make it a lot easier on yourself. A lot of the time we suffer from this inner mental "Civil War", and our minds become a battleground because we cannot make a decision and stick with it. We will do one thing for two weeks, and when we don't see results, we'll flip to the next method. This only causes confusion. A VIP woman must be ready, willing and able to live with any negative backlash for the decisions that she makes. Sadly enough, a lot of women have very weak and impotent decision-making muscles because we live out of fear of what other people will think of us. This is classic people pleasing syndrome. It's time to reclaim your VIP power and start making decisions that are best for you.

Grit and Elbow Grease:

Some people are not mentally tough because they don't want to do the hard work that goes along with success. They want microwave success. They want success to happen for them overnight. They want to have other people do the heavy lifting for them, and then they want to get the credit for it. That's the wrong way to go about it in life. You got to have grit. You must put the elbow grease into your work. You have to strengthen your mental backbone by being willing to do the work over and over again. Like in the past previous chapters I talked about mastering the basics. You must master the basics over and over again until it becomes second nature for you and easy. Then you build on top of that. The definition of grit almost perfectly describes the qualities that almost every successful person possesses. And yes, mental toughness builds the foundations for long-term success.

So, in order to become successful, and mentally tough, we must fall in love with working hard.

Stop the Back and Forth: You actually can drain yourself mentally. Quiet the chatter in your head. It's been scientifically proven that 49% percent of the time our mind wanders off. What the heck are we wondering about? Stay Focused. Don't drain your brain power. To be mentally tough you have to always be asking yourself "what am I thinking about right now?" and "What do I need to be focusing on right here right now?" Your mind is like a slippery fish, or like a slippery bar of soap that can just fly out of your grasp. Wrangle it back in by always asking yourself "what do I need to be thinking about right now? What is top priority?" This will help you to stop the back and forth in your mind, because when you take two steps forward, and two steps back you're just in the same place. I see that a lot in mental patterns. So make a decision. Stick with it. And look forward to it.

Look 10 Steps Ahead, Like a Chess Game: In life, in order to be mentally tough and when, we've got to look 10 steps in advance. Some of the best chess players always look ten steps ahead. It has proven to be effective when you begin a goal or a task with the end in mind. I'm going to be honest with you. I'm not an avid chess player. But, I've always admired those that have had the mental acuity, the genius, and the mental power to become a master at this "sport". It's all based on strategy and seeing how the future can play out by making one bad or good move. This is where your mental toughness comes into play. You see, if you want a certain outcome in your life, you have to make tough decisions every day to get there. So, as your transformational coach, wanting you to evoke your VIP power, I must train you to see your life as if it is a chess game.

We can actually take this very intense game of intelligence and apply its principles to our life in order to be successful and more mentally tough. This helps us to create the success that we desire and deserve.

If you ever played chess, you can see that the principles in this game often resemble real life and offer valuable insight. Here's my Chess Principle list for you to consider so you can enjoy a successful VIP life! Remember its more about strategy than it is motivation!

Chess Principle #1: Sometimes you don't have to move forward.

It's funny how sometimes doing nothing is the best option. Some of the best world champion chess players have "waiting moves". If you don't have any choices that you like right now, just simply wait!

Chess Principle #2 Claim Stake in as Many "Open Files", or Opportunities, That You Can

In chess, the columns and rows of the boards are called files. Open files are when no chess piece has staked its claim in that area. So an objective in chess is that you want to control as many open files by placing pieces at the top and bottom or left to right of these files. In other words, you want to place pieces there. Life is the same way. Look for these opportunities. When an opportunity presents itself to you, dominate it! Or as they say in chess, set yourself in it. I like to say stake your claim. Put your VIP flag there. Honestly opportunities rarely happen if you don't look for them, or more importantly create them. So kick it up a notch, create these open files of opportunity in your life, and set yourself in them.

How do you do this? You network and make powerful connections. You navigate through the important people in your industry or field. You connect with other "Power Players". It takes mental toughness to do this. Sometimes opportunities will be rare and you have to be patient and have the mental strength to be persistent. In other seasons of your life, you will have many opportunities coming in all at once. That takes another type of mental toughness. Being able to sift through the countless opportunities that come your way and really snap out the good ones.

Chess Principle #3 Haste Makes Waste.

It takes a seasoned player to know when to move, and also never to move too quickly. Probably one of the most important skills you can learn in chess and in life is not moving too quickly. How can you apply this chess principal in your life? Patience is a vehicle that can drive you very far in life. We must train our mental toughness, by being at peace with delaying our instant gratification.

As a VIP, I want you to focus more on the quality of your moves, and less on time. It takes mental toughness not to rush through any moves in life, think it through, and also utilize your time more wisely by not moving rapidly through it. Exercise your patience. And know that haste makes waste.

Chess Principle #4 Expand Your Options

In life, we will always have more alternatives than we think we have. So, always look for the alternative moves. How? Expand your options. Too often in life we come to a crossroads where we need to make a decision, and we will see it as a good move, and we want to move forward immediately. Instead, give yourself the gift of time and look for even better options. When you broaden the selection of choices you have, you also give yourself the gift of a real good choice among other alternatives. You see a VIP woman knows that she's never stuck, and there's always more than what meets the eye. You have more options at your fingertips than meets the eye. Opportunities are everywhere, but we we originally might not see them.

Case in point: one of my VIP clients was sick and tired of her job. It was either she kept working like a slave, or she quit. She didn't see anything else that she could do then those two options. We then did a coaching consultation and we started masterminding. I asked her about her daily schedule. I also asked her what her passions were and what she loved to do. She loved pets and she always would walk her dogs in the morning. I then triggered her in a positive way. I asked her how she can make money doing what she loves? I also asked her how she could make money doing what she already does? So she started a dog-walking side hustle which ended up being very lucrative. I took it a step further and I asked her with all these new business relationships she's created with these busy dog owners what else could she do? She had a background in administrative work. I asked her to get her resume together and hand it to all of her current dog owner clients. So, after walking their dogs, she would do VIP administrative and secretarial work as well as running errands for these very busy professionals. She loved what she did. She could work the hours into her schedule and she wasn't chained to a desk. Now to me that's a major chess move of VIP success!

Chess Principle #4 You Must Occupy Your Own Center

In order for you to truly be a VIP, and to own your life, you must own the center of your life. Chess players are always aiming at the center of the board. By aiming at the middle of the chessboard, this invites early confrontation ahead of time to occupy the important squares in life. The important squares of life such as your finances, your health, your personal freedom, love, and so forth. So, always aim at the center of your life. Make sure you are 100% owning the core of your life. This way you have truly set yourself up for success. You cannot build your life, or take it to the next level, if you do not already own the center blocks of your life.

Case in point: My mother did not own the center of her life. It was hinged on my dad. She was financially dependent upon him. She did not have self-love or self-respect. Therefore she sought out love and respect from him which he never gave her. Therefore she went into a downward spiral into emotional eating, thus gaining weight, and playing the blame game, she became the victim very quickly of a poorly set up lifestyle situation. I saw my mother suffer first hand at the hands of my father, as she was stuck in a marriage that was loveless, and had no financial support. Sadly enough, I see a lot of women falling into that trap. So don't shove yourself into the corner of your own chess board surrounded by non-supportive chess pieces of the opposing side.

Chess Principle #5 Protect Your Queen!

If you use your Queen's Pawn carelessly, many times you will end up in a bad power position.

Focus on achieving long-term success outcomes, and be wary of the "Quick Fix" results that often give the illusion of progress. Don't buy into the fake notion that being busy is being productive, this way of thinking can quickly lead to burn out. So, take care of your queen, and protect her; never putting her in a position that will leave her vulnerable, powerless, and overexposed.

So, there you have it. It's so amazing how the game of chess can very easily be a powerful metaphor for applying winning VIP strategies in your life. This helps you to set yourself up for success by using mental toughness and looking at your moves 10 steps in advance.

NOTES:

_____

_____

_____

_____

_____

_____

_____

_____

_____

_____

_____

_____

_____

_____

_____

_____

_____

Open Letter to Hard Work by Jennifer Nicole Lee:

Dear hard work,

I love you! I appreciate you! You never talk back to me, and you're always giving me ten times more results than what I put into you. I know that there's no substitute for you. Hard work, you're always in my corner. I know that the harder I work, the luckier I get! The word luck stands for "Labor Under Correct Knowledge." I love you so much because of I work hard, and earn whatever I desire, it is mine and nobody can take it away from me. So, hard work, we are intertwined, and are inseparable. I love you hard work, because you don't allow me to cheapen my integrity by crying victim, and blaming others. I love you hard work because it adds virtue to my characteristics. When I work hard, it makes me a better person. I love you so much because when I work hard, nobody can ever say that I'm lazy, or that I take the easy way around, or that I microwave my success. Hard work, thank you for being my best friend, because when I show up, I'm actually showing off just how hard I work, shining a light on others that are taking it easy. Hard work, I love you because you don't allow any half steppin, or half ass work. You won't allow it. You see right through the BS. Hard work I love you because you give me energy. Yes it's true, the harder I work, the more energy I get. You helped me build my stamina and endurance and therefore my persistence and resiliency as well. Hard work, you always continue to raise the bar in my life. Others see me as a hard worker and that's a compliment to me. Thank you for being in my life, thank you for being my backbone, and thank you for giving me the intestinal fortitude to wake up and kick butt every day and never give up!

FUN WORK:

Now it's your turn to write your Open Letter to Hard Work! Please write it below:

_____

_____

_____

_____

_____

_____

_____

_____

_____

_____

_____

Emotional Strength

Women by nature are emotional beings. This is good because we are the nurturers, the caretakers, and those that give birth and raise our children. However it can backfire on us. We can let our emotions run us where we become powerless to them. In this section I'm going to teach you how to become emotionally stronger, and make your emotions work for you and not against you.

A common trait that I've heard many women complain about is that they get overwhelmed, anxious, worried, doubtful, jealous, and exhausted. These are common emotions. I'm going to help you remove these triggers, and also gain emotional stamina and increase your emotional IQ so that you are constantly evoking positive emotions instead of negative ones. Remember, 90% of the time women are eating emotionally. Emotional impulses that drive your appetite can only lead to unhealthy eating habits, and long-term weight gain and obesity.

The Flip: How do we gain control of negative emotions? It's simple. We flip them. I wrote about this in my first "Reclaim Your VIP Power Book" and also my countless coaching sessions and online Wellness platform at JNLVIP.com

If you get overwhelmed, flip it and say "I am so grateful that I am busy as being busy and productive is having a blessed, colorful, robust life of opportunity. I'm grateful that my cup runneth over!"

If you get anxious, flip it and say "I'm not anxious, I'm excited! I'm thrilled to see what the future holds for me! I'm growing through this situation. Thank you Universe for sending me this life lesson that I will get stronger from."

If you are worried, flip it and say "I don't live in fear, I live in faith! I know that my goals will be met. All things will work out for my good. I don't have to worry because I know that my higher power is with me and watching over me. I know that karma is real. Whoever is doing bad to me, it'll come back to them tenfold. All I need to do is get out of the way, let go, and simply let God. I just need to stay prayed up and I know miracles will happen! I believe it!'

If you are doubtful, flip it and say "I am certain of the outcome. I have conviction that all will work out in my honor. I am confident and I trust the journey. I'm so grateful I'm able to do all that I can in my power, and let go and let God".

If you are jealous, flip it and say "I'm excited for her. I'm not going to be jealous because jealousy is evidence of a lack of trust, confidence and belief in the greatness that I possess in my own life. I'm going to work twice as hard to achieve my goals so that I don't have to be jealous of anyone.

If you are exhausted, flip it and say "I'm so grateful that I have a lot on my plate. God never gives me more than I can handle. I know that the burdens and the time restraints I'm experiencing now will only make me a better person in the long run. I'm learning how to budget my time, focus my mental energy, and not allow the small things in life to drain me. I'm now going to wipe the slate clean, focus on what is important, and leave the rest.

In closing, as you can see you are the master of your emotions, not the other way around. Once you nail self-mastery of your emotions, everything else is easy! Make your emotions your best friend, and if you catch yourself sliding down and into a negative emotional track, get yourself back on track by replacing them with positive ones! In other words raise your vibration.

Build a Body that Is Stronger than Ever

The theme of September is STRONG! There's no greater gift that you can give yourself than a strong body! We all agree that there is a mind, body and spirit connection. With that being said, we must strengthen our body in order to also have a strong mental space, which then overflows into emotional well-being. So that every rep you're taking physically, and every workout, you're actually strengthening your mental space and also your emotions. What a beautiful trilogy!

Here are my top tips on how to build a stronger body. No matter how strong, or weak, you feel now, you can only get stronger!

Lift Heavier- Just to be clear, no, you will not end up looking like Arnold Schwarzenegger! You will end up looking even leaner! I call it TNT, short for tight and toned. You may initially "gain weight" when you start lifting heavier, but remember muscle weighs more than fat. So, don't get too stuck on the scale. Remember the more muscle you have, the stronger your metabolism will be. So, keep lifting! Don't allow your muscles to hit a plateau.

Less Rest In Between Sets-. How can you continue to push yourself to be stronger? By resting less in between sets. When you rest less in between sets, you will increase your endurance and stamina. You're going to have that "get up and go power" all day long. This is a mental tip. This is why I use a timer in our online workouts at www.JNLVIP.com When you hear that 30-second timer beep, you know it's time to rest. But then only allow yourself 10 to 12 seconds to go into the next round of cardio or weights.

Up The Quality of Your Rest & Recover Days! Taking a rest day does not mean putting your feet up and eating donuts. It means active recovery. It means foam rolling to work out the lactic acid. A massage with a deep tissue focus to release knots and pain. Epsom salt baths to also help in muscle soreness, muscle fatigue, and recovery quicker. Make sure you get your supplements in as well such as your BCAAs and creatine. Don't be lazy and blow it all off with a huge cheat day. Let's be smart here.

<u>Make Sure You Eat Enough Protein:</u> You can't build a house without cement blocks, wood, or hammer and nails. You got to have the right building blocks in order to also repair and build muscle. So, make sure you eat an adequate amount of protein. For an active VIP woman, it is suggested 7-1 grams per pound of lean mass.

Now that we covered some VIP principles on how to build a strong body, lets continue to the subject of falling back in love with ourselves!

Fall in Love

Oscar Wilde said "To love oneself is the beginning of a life-long romance." And I agree!

Love is the most powerful emotion in the world. Love heals all. Love for others is actually a commandment in the Bible. We must love ourselves in order to progress. So in this section, I will be covering how to fall back in love with yourself, how to fall back in love with life, and how to fall back in love with your soulmate or spouse.

How to fall back in love with yourself:

You must gain a deeper appreciation for your own worth and capabilities. When you genuinely like yourself, and you even enjoy spending time alone, this means that you have fallen in love with yourself. This is extremely healthy.

Sadly enough, society puts a lot of emphasis on the romantic love of a significant other. Yes, it's important to find true love that you can share with another human being. However, you must first master the art of self-love in order to have a healthy loving relationship with another person. Another person can never fill in an inner void or solve all of your problems. You have to do that for yourself.

Keep a Running List of Your Accomplishments

Our memories are wired to remember harsh incidences where we failed. So instead of making a "to do" list, why don't we make a list of all your accomplishments. Let's bring to the forefront of your memory all the wonderful things that you have done in the past. This will refresh your memory and showcase just how amazing you are, that's sparking the self-love flames. You should always keep a running list of all your accomplishments because it has numerous benefits. When you look over your list, you will be reminded just how capable and valuable you are, it'll show you how much you achieve, and also help you feel a sense of confidence and respect for yourself. Yes, when you feel good about yourself, you will certainly love yourself more.

Date Yourself

You are the best company you can never give yourself. Enjoy a lunch out, take yourself to dinner. What's your favorite movie, read your favorite book. Spending time with yourself, doing your favorite things, will increase a healthy relationship with yourself and also raise up your vibration and inner peace.

View Yourself Through Loving Eyes

To help you focus on your good qualities, instead of brushing them under the carpet, or taking your talents for granted, try this powerful exercise. Think of your spouse, child, your loving relative, or even your best friend. Next, picture that person next to you looking at you. Now, see yourself through their eyes. How do they describe you? What do they see? Why do they love you? You see, you are extremely lovable! So on the days you're feeling down and out, remember to view yourself through the eyes of someone who loves you.

Engage in Positive Self-Talk

No more negative self-talk. It ends today and it ends forever. How ironic is it that we would speak nicer to a complete stranger, or even a family member that we don't even like. But we will sabotage our own success by inflicting negative self-talk onto ourselves. Flip it! Instead of negative self-talk, enjoy positive self-talk. Once you catch yourself talking negative to yourself, stop riding your traps then flip it. Replace all negative talk with positive! It is that simple!

Imagine Yourself as a Little Girl, A Younger Version of You

Take the time to visualize yourself as a little girl. How would you talk to her? How would you treat her? You of course would show her extra love, extra support, and extra guidance. Do the same thing with your grown self. It's that simple.

To give you a snapshot, and to break it down into bite-sized action steps, here are some of my top tips and VIP Keys to Success to kick start this fierce love affair with yourself! Let's rekindle this romance asap!

1. Know that you are more than enough.

2. Don't wait for others to give you what you need. Instead, give it to yourself.

3. Embrace both your strengths and your weaknesses.

4. Root for yourself.

5. Be your own cheerleader.

6. Even if nobody else is, be in your own corner.

7. Be your own biggest fan. Never in a cocky way, but believe in yourself.

8. Don't beat yourself up if you make a mistake. Be gentle with yourself when you fail.

9. It's okay to do things alone. Be comfortable with doing things alone.

How to Fall Back in Love with Life

Faith It Til' You Make It

Falling back in love with life is really a shift in mindset. As I like to say in my coaching program at www.JNLVIP.com, you have to "Faith it until you make it". Never fake anything. It's like living a lie! Take the F for faith and put it back in the word lie and you will get LIFE!

So use the power of Faith to add love, zest, passion, excitement, and enjoyment back into your life! Use the power of faith to transform the everyday average moment from blah to so amazing. Know that there's a miracle around every corner. Expect blessings to happen every day. Know that divine intervention is real. Know that God has got your back and know that you have Guardian Angels wherever you go. Once you start looking at life like a never-ending journey of divine surprises, you will wake up with excitement not even needing an alarm clock.

Practice Gratitude: When you start each day with an attitude of gratitude, you automatically shift into a state of love and when you're in a state of love you naturally attract all good things your way.

Be Willing to Receive Love: Don't shun compliments when they are directed at you. Accept a helping hand from your friends when they offer it to you. Allow yourself to receive gifts. When you allow yourself to be loved in these small ways, watch how easier it is to accept your own love from yourself too.

Give Yourself Gifts: Isn't it funny how we are willing to give gifts to others? But we won't give gifts to ourselves? Did you have your eye on that ring? Get it for yourself! Did you have the urge to take yourself on a beautiful trip? Save up for it and do it! Whatever is on your bucket list for yourself, make it a point to manifest it and bring it into reality.

View Your Wellness Journey As More than Just Losing Weight: When you stress yourself out, to become a certain number on the scale, or certain dress size, to meet that does not constitute being healthy. You must look at your health through a holistic lens. Health isn't just about drinking your green smoothies, or getting your workouts in, even though it is also about that, true health means that you are taking care of yourself, addressing your mind, body and spirit. When you fail to make time for self-care, it means failing to make time for your overall sense of well-being.

Now that we have addressed the importance of self-love, there's many of you that are in relationships and you might feel stuck or that your love is burned out. In the next section we are going to revive and rekindle the love that you still have inside for your soulmate.

How to Fall Back in Love with Your Soulmate or Spouse.

The honeymoon is over and reality sets in. Maybe the love dwindled down to a small little flicker of a once roaring bonfire. Can you fall back in love with your soulmate? You absolutely can!

I believe in the power of love. I believe in miracles. Some relationships are not meant to last. But then when you meet your soulmate, and you dedicate your life to each other, you might hit a rough patch. However, with the right coaching, and VIP success Keys, you can revive the power of your true love.

Forgiveness: If you are in a healthy relationship, but the love needs to be revived, and you want it to work, you must be willing to forgive any wrongdoing in the past. Forgiveness is one of the most powerful success keys ever. Forgive and be willing to wipe the slate clean and press the reset button. Some challenges that couples face in their relationships can turn out to be blessings in disguise. You can use them as tools, and action bumper plates, on what not to do next time, only making your relationship stronger in the future.

Reminisce on the old times: Taking a walk down memory lane can be very therapeutic. It can conjure up those butterflies you once had in your stomach during your first kiss. He can bring up those happy, joyful, indescribable feelings of excitement that you got when you first met.

Bring that energy to the forefront into your current relationship and watch the sparks fly!

Create a New Memory Bank: Do new things together. Why is this important? A lot of times in lengthy relationships, you get stuck reliving the past and doing the same things over and over again. That can get boring and redundant. One of the main things you may be missing in your relationship is the element of surprise. As the years roll by, it's very easy to settle into a comfortable routine where you know exactly what to expect day after day, week after week. Maybe it's time for a little variety and to spice things up. Don't be afraid to do new things together. Whether it's finding a new sport or hobby, or even having a holiday together. Getting away and enjoying some alone time is a great way to draw closer to each other. And most importantly, make it fun!

Now that we covered all types of love from self-love, falling back in love with life, and falling back in love with our significant other, you will experience magic and miracles on a daily level that will blow your mind! So, let's turn up the love! In the notes section below, please write what you found most powerful and what you want to work on:

_____

_____

_____

_____

_____

_____

_____

_____

_____

_____

_____

_____

_____

_____

_____

_____

_____

_____

_____

_____

_____

Fall Forward in Faith-Throw it Off a Cliff and See What Happens

As we continue to celebrate the theme of fall, I want to focus on the notion of falling forward and also failing forward.

In my VIP success book, I don't believe there is such a thing as failure, only results. When we "fail forward", we get to see firsthand what not to do the next time and what we must do better.

Failing forward is leveraging mistakes. When we make realistic assessments of risks and accept that failure is part of the process, we understand that actually falling forward is an investment in human success. I call this throwing things off a cliff and seeing what happens. Sometimes we get paralysis by over-analysis. When we throw things off a cliff and see what happens, we stop being scared and allow ourselves to fail forward and are able to assess the results. Remember highly successful people are the ones who failed the most.

There is a famous quote about feelings that goes something like this, "Fail early, fail fast, and fail often". The more you fail, and the faster you recover, the more successful you will become.

And to be more clear, failing is not a mistake. A mistake is an error, a blunder, while failure is a state or condition of not meeting a desirable or intended objective which is the opposite of success.

So here are my top tips on how to fail forward:

Try and try again. Don't be afraid to try, and if you don't get the desired outcome, try again. In other words, never give up.

Be in a Constant State of Learning: I'm going to be honest. The only way I learn is by doing. Therefore, if I do something and I fail at it, then at least I learned. There's textbook learning, and then there's the real "School of Hard Knocks", where reality can give you a PhD in experience.

Learn from other people's mistakes: The great news is you don't need to make all the mistakes. In the information age, we can do a simple Google search and learn a lot from other people's past failures and attempts. We can apply what worked for them, and as well as learn what did not work for them.

FAIL stands for "First Attempt In Learning"

If you fail, never give up because F.A.I.L stands for "first attempt in learning". End is not the end, in fact, E.N.D stands for "effort never dies". If you get NO as an answer, remember N.O. means "Next Opportunity"-Quote by **A.P.J. Abdul Kalam**

So in Closing, remember that there's no such thing as failure, only results, and these results are useful tools to help you know what to do and more importantly what not to do the next time around. So, don't stop failing forward.

Fun Work: look to the past. What did you fail on? How did you learn from this experience? What made you never give up and move forward?

_____

_____

_____

_____

_____

_____

_____

_____

_____

_____

_____

_____

_____

Looking back at the past, what major mistake ended up being a major success breakthrough in disguise?

_____

_____

_____

_____

_____

_____

_____

_____

_____

_____

_____

_____

_____

_____

In closing Chapter 9 for September, what type of memories do you plan on creating in the future? How do you plan on winning more in life? How can you become a VIP architect for your future?

NOTES FOR CHAPTER 9:

_____

_____

_____

_____

_____

_____

_____

_____

_____

_____

_____

_____

CHAPTER 10

OCTOBER: HARVEST SEASON, LATE SEASON CROPS. LIVE IN FAITH, NOT FEAR

Delayed Doesn't Mean Denied-All In Gods Time

How to Stop Living in Fear What Looks Scary Really Isn't All That Scary-Seeing Through the Smoke and Mirrors of Life

How to Outsmart Winter Weight Gain

Welcome to October! What a beautiful time of the year. As the leaves continue to turn into beautiful vibrant hues and gorgeous colors; gearing up for winter, we celebrate all of our "late season crops".

What are late season crops? I'm using this powerful metaphor to represent all of the hard work that you put into this past year, and how it is now paying off. Or on a broader and much larger scale, it is extremely helpful to look back at your life and notice all of your hard work throughout the past years. It is marvelous to see the seeds that you planted long ago now manifest into the results that you've always wanted.

As your life coach and friend, I know that it is easy to get frustrated when you are living a focused and disciplined life and you don't get the results that you want. It can be downright discouraging. And I know that at times you may want to give up, quit and throw in the towel. But this is where the power of patience comes into play. In this chapter, I'm going to help you understand the importance of being persistent, and also patient.

Delayed Doesn't Mean Denied-All in God's Time-
Patience is not the ability to wait, but the ability to keep a good attitude while waiting. Patience and perseverance have a magical effect. They make challenges and obstacles vanish.

It's not only important to never give up. Never giving up is essential to being successful in all areas of your life! I know that on the journey in life we can get discouraged if we don't see results fast enough. I know that delay tactics are a favorite deception of the enemy because he seeks to trip us up by filling us up with doubt. When we don't see results, it's almost as if the enemy wants us to believe that we will never achieve our dreams. But that's not true. Maybe your goals are to get out of financial debt. Maybe your goal is to get healthy and out of sickness. Maybe your goals are to finally get the success you deserve in your career, but you still fall short financially. You see, the enemy wants you to think that you are hopeless, forgotten, and going nowhere fast. But again that's a lie! The enemy wants you to think that God is not interested in your needs or fulfilling the promises that He's already made to you.

I'm going to be upfront with you here. You don't need to be a holier-than-thou church-goer to make miracles happen in your life. All you need to do is ask, believe by having faith and you shall receive. So take the time to truly look back and see if you've asked for what you desired. Have you gone into prayer, or meditation, and clearly asked for what you are seeking to manifest? And if you haven't, start today! Build this relationship with your higher power. It's the most beautiful relationship you can nurture, grow, and also benefit from.

<u>All in God's Time</u>   Okay! So, you've asked and now you are ready to receive; but nothing is happening. You can't seem to get the traction in your life that you need in order to get the results that you are yearning for. But remember, just because it is delayed doesn't mean that you are being denied. Think about this example: You have a young child, she wants to drive a car but can't even see over the steering wheel. She's begging, crying, throwing a tantrum, and is trying to convince you that she can drive a car across town to go visit her friend.

You are her guardian, having to make decisions and choices to keep her safe. And because of age and experience, you know more than her. You know that if she gets into the car, she won't be able to drive it and eventually will most likely wreck and have an accident that could be extremely detrimental to her health and physically harm her. This is the same with you and your goals, and how God sees if you are ready or not. So as your transformational coach, my advice to you is to get as prepared as you can. Continue to work on yourself and sharpen your skill sets. Continue to work on your goals and do all that is in your power to move forward in your VIP life! Keep tapping into the strength of your faith in order to get ready to receive your desires of your heart and the manifestations of your dreams. Once God sees that you are 100% ready, the blessings that He has assigned to you will be bestowed upon you. I've seen this time and time again in my own personal life. We must prepare ourselves as much as possible, and then let go and let God.

Also timing is everything. If you're off by a split-second, you can either make a homerun, or a strike. So trust in God's timing. He wants what is best for you and will bless you when the time is right. And yes, God wants you to never strike out, and will set you up to always hit home runs with impeccable timing!

Keep Your Eye on the Prize

In life, your goals and accomplishments are not going to be served to you on a silver platter just because you asked for them. Once you get clear on what your goals are, and you put forth a strong work ethic, doing something every day to work towards your goals, you must keep your eye on the prize. I love this powerful metaphor because the ebb and flow of life will knock you down. The big waves and winds of life's biggest storms can knock you over; but you must always get up and never give up. Keeping your eye on the prize will help you become more persistent, resilient and give you the VIP Power to never give up on your goals.

October is the fall season where we celebrate Halloween. This holiday is where all the ghouls and goblins come out and the scary costumes and decorations are put on display. Sadly enough, some of us are living in this scary Halloween season all year long because we are living in fear. In this section I'm going to cover how you can overcome living in daily fear.

How to Stop Living in Fear

Let's face it, we live in a culture of fear. Fear has been rampant in our news, especially with the coronavirus. Fear of catching it, fear of getting sick, and yes, the worst fear of all, dying from it. However, that's not the only fear that we all face. We face the fear of aging, public speaking, asserting ourselves, making decisions, being intimate, being alone, pollution, and fear of being judged. Basically, you name it, there's a fear for it. How do we get over fear? Keep reading and I'll show you how!

Feel the Fear and Do it Anyways

Remember, a VIP woman is a fearless spirit, and is full of faith! I personally have learned how to move from a place of pain, paralysis, depression, and indecision, to one of enthusiasm, positive action, personal power, endless energy, and with having strong decision making muscles.

What really is fear anyways? F.E.A.R. stands for " false evidence appearing real". Therefore, if we understand that what we're hearing is not even reality, we have the strength, courage, and confidence to move from a hopeless position of fear to a powerful one of faith.

Start to Trust Yourself.

There are many scary twists and fearful turns in the journey of life. You must have more confidence in yourself and less fear in the unstable circumstances that happen in all of our lives. Maybe you failed yourself in the past, leaving you with a subconscious notion that you cannot trust yourself. Well it's time to flip it, and flush it! Your past does not have to dictate your future. I'm here to remind you that you have conquered too many hard things and slayed too many goals to even start listing off here. So, go ahead and give yourself some credit. You must believe in yourself, even when no one else does. Challenge yourself to believe in your own capabilities and you can become powerful beyond your wildest dreams!

Prayer is a powerful VIP tool that I mentioned many times in my writings and teachings. And no, you don't need to be a nun or a Mother Theresa to enjoy the power of prayer. For me, the power of prayer is like using the magic of intuition. Prayer is like telephoning God. Your intuition is when God is calling you. So, we must harness the power of intuition. We must cultivate, grow, and nurture our sixth sense. Meditation can help with this. When you quiet your mind, those small nudges from the universe, the little whispers that are extremely loud and the clarity will come to you. One powerful VIP method of cultivating intuition is saying to yourself "in the morning I will know exactly what to do." Ideas will flash before you! You will gain immediate clarity and direction. Move swiftly on your intuition when it nudges you, as soon as you take obedient action, the next move will lead you to the next, and it's not until you're further down the road in your life and into the promise of your future that you can truly recognize all of the miracles that have been happening in your life all along.

Seeing Through the Smoke and Mirrors of Life, Learn How to See Through the Illusions

It's horrible that even in the self-help industry, many so-called gurus and experts profit off of the fears of many people. They capitalized off of your fear of not being financially successful, or not being in shape, or having a lackluster resume. So please be wary of all of the smoke and mirrors in life. These experts puff themselves up, with imaginary accolades, awards, and often give themselves too much credit. They over-charge and underdeliver, "financially raping" their clients, and essentially robbing them blind. You, my VIP friend, have seen through the illusions. No more being a victim. No more being a pawn. You are now making your own power moves. Rise up and out of the smoke and mirrors in your life, and journey beyond the fake illusions of life. As some would say, your third eye is now wide open.

For example, during the Halloween season, have you ever gone through a haunted house? The ones that were full of smoke machines and mirrors that confused you? These are all illusions that will knock you off your path, scare you silly, and push you back into an emotional corner of fear. Even though these haunted houses are a seasonal activity, sadly enough life can be like this all year round. Please watch the news headlines as there's a lot of smoke and mirrors. Please see through the illusions of your neighbors and their false sense of security just because they are showing off that their grass is greener on their side. You must stay steadfast in your goals, and not be riddled with fear when focusing on what is best for you. You must have thick skin and not allow all the smoke, mirrors, and illusions of life to make you feel "less than worthy" or shove you into a small box of fear. Remember that these are all illusions.

Reclaim Your VIP Power By Assigning Meaning to Everything Around You

You are actually the one assigning meaning to everything around you. For example, say your best friend got a promotion, she got a mortgage and moved into her new home, and is now a home owner, she finally got down to a size 4, she's now dating the man of her dreams. You might feel a little jealous, or feel less than her. However, you shouldn't! Remember these are all smoke and mirrors. At the end she might hate her job and it could end up being a "work prison". Her new home might become a burden to her and a money pit with unforeseeable repairs. She might in a year bounce back up to a size 12. The man of her dreams may end up becoming the monster of her nightmares. Therefore, you should never be jealous of anyone else. Never assign bad meanings to events in your life. Remember, be pronoia and believe that all things happen for your benefit! Flip it!

And furthermore, your friend just may be in a due season of winning after many consecutive losses. We never know just how much others may have suffered or sacrificed to be in the positions that they are in. This is why it's so important to never covet the blessings of others. You have no idea what appears to be a blessing from the outside looking in is really a burden. And you have no idea the weight of the burden that had to be carried in order for them to have access to these major blessings. Trust in the timing of your life, be happy for others and know that your time is coming.

God can never run out of blessings. He is so abundant, there is room for you to be blessed too. You have everything you need. So, take everything with a grain of salt, take a deep inhale and exhale knowing that you can trust yourself, you're going to see through the illusions of life, and yes, keep your eye on the prize.

FUN WORK: Use the space below to brainstorm and master mind on how you are going to get through the scary seasons of life that challenge you.

_____

_____

_____

_____

_____

_____

_____

_____

_____

How to Out Smart Winter Weight Gain

Okay VIPs, it's time to get real! The days are getting shorter, the weather is getting colder, and the hectic, high-calorie, holiday season is right around the corner. It's time to get prepared to outsmart the winter weight gain!

The "Holiday Food Wars" start at Halloween and go all the way until New Years Eve. The Halloween candy! Thanksgiving meals full of mashed potatoes, macaroni and cheese, apple pie, and chocolate chip cookies! Then Christmas and the main holiday season with drinks, endless nibbles, cakes, cookies and celebration dinners. You know the holiday food wars are coming and coming in fast! So, we must prepare to win this winter weight gain war! First, let's get a little scientific! We need to fully comprehend why we gain weight in the winter and how we can resolve it. Below are some of my VIP fixes to zap winter weight gain fat in its tracks!

Not only is Santa Clause coming to town, so are a lot of additional pounds! Get this: on average, many gain a whopping 7-12 pounds during the holidays and usually their New Year's resolution to lose it only lasts about 2 weeks. This newly gained weight is then brought into the New Year as "new baggage"!

There are a lot of strikes against us such as cold weather, bundling up in multiple layers, food being the focus of many activities and also holiday stress! Let's dive in and take a closer look at all the numerous factors that play a part.

COLD WEATHER AND ITS ROLE IN WEIGHT GAIN

You heard it hundreds of times in one of the oldest Christmas carols: "the weather outside is frightful!" As we all know, sometimes it's just that much more pleasant to stay inside than to face the harsh cold weather outside.

We are almost forced to move less during these cold winter months, therefore making it harder to burn off the extra calories. In addition, the weather forces us to also wear big, bulky clothes allowing us to cover up our problem areas.

As the old adage goes, "out of sight, out of mind."

VIP FIT TIP: Place your swimsuit or favorite pair of jeans where you can see them every day! And try them on weekly! Our clothes should inspire us to take our wellness seriously. I mean, lets face it VIPS, we paid for our clothing, so why not wear them! Did you buy them so they can just sit in your closet? No! I remember a great story about Arnold Schwarzenegger who purposely would walk around in a cut off shirt, exposing his abs. He used this technique to continually remind himself to eat the right foods and always make working out a priority.

Use this strategy too: once a week, put on your swimsuit and take a good look. Use this tool to take a personal inventory of your problem areas, and what you need to work on. And no matter what the weather is outside, make sure you get your exercise in! This is why our VIP workouts work! We don't have to depend upon the weather, as we are set up for VIP success with our designated workout area in our homes.

Also, the physiological aspects of cold weather are powerful. For thousands of years, when the temperature dropped, it instantly triggers a survival aspect, thus urging us to want to eat more. It's a trick that our own mind plays on us.

When it's cold, we want to eat due to our survival mechanism which is deep in our human conditioning. We can combat this by using our food journal, making sure we eat every 2-3 hours, and using portion control.

Another helpful tip is to eat when we are at a level 7 or 8 on a scale of 1-10 for our hunger. This will keep our wild food cravings at bay. If you wait until you are starving, at a level 10, then you are setting yourself up for failure with an uncontrollable binge.

And check out this study: one study had 10 people in a colder room, and another set of 10 in another that was at a comfortable temperature. Both sets of people were fed the same meals at lunch. The study showed that the ones in the colder room ate more than the other set. This illustrates that colder weather does indeed cause people to eat more.

By understanding this phenomenon and planning your meals in advance, you will have much more control over your eating habits during the cold winter months.

VIP FIT TIP: Sip on hot herbal tea with a squeeze of lemon instead to keep your body temperature warm, thus warding off winter weight gain urges to eat.

FOOD IS THE FOCAL POINT OF MANY HOLIDAY GATHERINGS

Let's face it, when the holidays are here, food is the focal point of most social gatherings. Parties, get-togethers, and family dinners are all high food affairs with tons of tempting unhealthy choices. Also many people feel forced to eat to fit in and blend into the party. There are even some social instances when it may also be considered rude not to eat. We can combat this by making sure we eat beforehand and not arriving to the social function on an empty stomach. This will cut the urge to over indulge in high fat and high calorie treats.

Instead of focusing on the food at your next party, make sure you strike up conversations with your fellow friends. Concentrate on your networking and connecting at your holiday get togethers rather than just the food. If you really want to dig in, just remember the one golden rule of the holidays: "all things in moderation."

HOLIDAYS ARE A STRESSFUL TIME

Even with all the cheerful glee, the holidays can be a stressful time. We all have tons of "to-do's" with so little time to get it all done. It is plausible that during this season we are prone to more stress, leading to emotional eating as it soothes our nerves. Sometimes we get confused and we are triggered by our own emotions to eat even when we are not hungry, therefore packing on the pounds from this mindless eating.

To deter this, try scheduling a "detox" time where you can go and just deep breathe for at least 10 minutes. It will de-stress you and help you to not resort to food when you get over stressed.

Our VIP workouts are also a great stress reliever. Make sure you treat your workouts as important business meetings that you cannot be late to, cancel, or "call in sick" to, with the most important person in the world: YOU!

During the holidays, it may seem much easier to forget about exercising all together until the New Year, but hang on! Make sure you schedule your workouts in advance and make them happen. Getting to your VIP workouts during the holidays will keep you less stressed and more balanced, therefore making your holiday season just that much more enjoyable!

OVERSCHEDULED CALENDARS

My solution for all of those who cannot find the time to work out is to: "put yourself back on your to-do list!" Yes, agreed – there's too much to do during the holidays, such as running errands, traveling, and shopping for presents.

We can use the excuse that we don't have time to exercise, but if you really make it a goal, you can always find the time. Shift your mindset from "I have to exercise," to "I get to exercise," and your body will take action! Look forward to your VIP workouts as a perfect solution to actually creating more time, as you will have more "get-up-and-go" energy just from working out. It's just as important as getting everything else done.

As you see, many have problems with Winter weight gain. Use these easy guidelines and you will find yourself enjoying a more balanced and healthier holiday season.

MAKE FRIENDS AGAIN WITH YOUR MEASURING CUPS-PRACTICE PORTION CONTROL

If there is one "Golden rule" to the holiday season, it is "All things in moderation." If you crave your Aunt Sue's famous pumpkin pie, then have a small slice that you can savor. Make every bite count!

I am not here to take all the fun out of the holidays for you, however if you want to maintain your physique you must work smarter not harder. Don't be like a "gerbil on a wheel," going nowhere fast by eating out of control and then going to the gym. Remember what is true: it's 20% exercise and 80% nutrition. If you keep this in mind, you won't go and blow your entire food plan by overeating this holiday season.

BE A SMARTER CHEF

Learn how to make "concoctions" where you tweak all of your favorite recipes, by taking out all the unnecessary fat and calories. I love to take my mom's old fashioned Italian recipes, and make them higher in protein and much leaner. You too can do the same with your recipes. Instead of shortening or oil, you can use applesauce when you bake. Take out all salt when it's not needed. And when you are cooking with eggs, take out the yolks. It's just that simple to be a smarter chef!

DON'T BE A PERFECTIONIST. RATHER, BE PERSISTENT

By banishing the "all or nothing" mentally towards your VIP lifestyle, you will be able to reach your goals and maintain them much easier. Therefore focus on not being perfect, but rather being persistent. If you can't work out for an entire hour and a half, then go for 30 minutes. At least you will be able to squeeze in abs and cardio and your body will thank you for it!

STAY ACTIVE

Yes, the holidays are about spending time with family and friends and not locking yourself up in the weight room. Therefore remember to keep moving and to open your mind for other ways to get your workout in with your family. In addition to your main VIP workouts, make sure to work in your "VIP fitness snacks"!

After dinner, go for a brisk walk to get fresh blood and oxygen circulating to all the cells in your body, or in the morning, enjoy a VIP workout while your family and friends are getting organized for the day. Make every minute of your day count by utilizing free moments to pick up a set of dumbbells and then pumping out a couple of sets. You will get energized and feel just that much better.

And most importantly, don't give up! Fitness is not a one-time event that you do once and forget about. Your VIP Fitness journey is to be enjoyed, one day at a time! Make the process fun and enjoyable. By doing this, you will be more likely to stick with it. Remember, you too can have a healthy and happy holiday season without gaining all the weight!

NOTES FOR CHAPTER 10:

_____

_____

_____

_____

_____

_____

_____

_____

_____

_____

_____

_____

_____

_____

_____

_____

_____

CHAPTER 11

NOVEMBER: NO-VEMBER! THE MONTH OF THANKSGIVING, AND HOW TO SET HEALTHY LIMITS & KINDLY ENFORCE YOUR BOUNDARIES

Time Management Tips for Managing Your Time Optimally

November truly is the month of Thanksgiving! We are going to give thanks for all our blessings, miracles, divine intervention and guidance that has helped us create the most amazing and beautiful life. We're also going to give thanks for the hardships that we've been able to overcome and be strengthened by. You see, the reason why you're reading this right now is that you have overcome so many trials and tribulations. We must raise up our gratitude vibration and celebrate in the spirit of Thanksgiving!

Setting healthy boundaries can be very challenging for us. We feel bad if we don't help others. Let me explain. Now there's a difference between helping others, and then being used and mistreated and taken advantage of. In this chapter we are going to learn to say NO in NO-vember!

We will also cover the power of time management and how to make time work for you so that you are no longer a slave to time! Okay VIPs, LET'S DO THIS!

Thanksgiving! The Power of Being Grateful

As you know by now, I put a lot of emphasis on the power of gratitude. This month we celebrate Thanksgiving. No matter what your beliefs are or how you feel about the holiday, we all need to come together and give thanks for all of our blessings, prosperity, health and abundance. You see, when you give thanks, you minimize negativity instantly! It truly is a VIP superpower.

Okay, you're not convinced? There's actually science that backs up the power of gratitude. When you are grateful, it's like exploding the bliss center of your brain, igniting your feel good positive vibes! How cool is this? Being thankful and expressing appreciation can lower blood pressure, increase energy and happiness, reduce depression, and even let you live a longer and healthier life!

Want to get "high?" I don't do any kind of drugs and I don't even drink! Those are bad for you! But my VIP program gives us all this beautiful natural high! Being grateful also increases the feel-good neurotransmitters serotonin and dopamine and helps you ward off those negative thoughts that can cause you to go into a downward spiral. So make sure you "get high" daily with your workouts, getting proper rest, and also eating lean, clean and green meals!

Why Being Grateful is your Secret Weapon and Super VIP Power

Ralph Waldo Emerson said it best! "Cultivate the habit of being grateful for every good thing that comes to you, and to give thanks continuously. Since all things have contributed to your advancement, you should include all things in your gratitude." I personally could not agree more with this quote. Being grateful surely is a super VIP Power!

VIP Rule to Long Term Success? JUST BE GRATEFUL!

"Can you just be grateful?" You heard your mom say it when you were a little kid and you were probably acting out and throwing a tantrum for something you wanted. You would hear your mother say just be happy with what you have. I'm going to be honest with you, I did not like hearing that when I was little. But, when I grew up and matured, I finally realized that I had to be happy with what I had in order to receive more. That was the switch that was flipped! I cracked my code. When I started being grateful for what I had, I started receiving more. When you're grateful, you are appreciative of what you have, therefore helping you to attract more.

VIP FACT: Research has found countless "brain hacks" and neurological reasons why people can improve their daily lives from this "easy-to-do" practice of expressing thanks for our lives, even during challenging times.

Why Being Grateful is a Magnet for What You Want

It's all about energy. And the stronger the positive energy you have, the stronger the magnetic pull you will create. When you have a ferocious amount of gratitude, on the level that can move mountains, you can literally pull and attract anything you desire in your life. When you are grateful, you are putting a psychic demand on the universe, and everything you want and desire will come your way! When you are grateful, divine intervention is pulled to the forefront of your life. The only result and outcome is for you to get exactly what your heart desires, or something even better. So what is my point? Just be grateful!

What is the Opposite of Being Grateful? Think about it. Choose: would you rather be beautiful, with a fabulous aura, glowing from the inside out with gratitude? Or be stressed, with a negative scowl on your face, always looking miserable and putting out this negative vibe that nobody wants to be around? Let's be real here. We've seen those women who are miserable. They have such a horrible nasty look on her face. Who wants to be like that? I would hate to look at myself in the mirror and see just how miserable I was! Plus you get wrinkles quicker that way! So don't frown and turn your frown upside down into a smile, I promise it'll be worth your while!

How to Be More Grateful

Okay, by now you are convinced that being grateful is a magic wand to creating a happy life, abundance, and endless opportunities of joy. But, how can you get into the groove of being grateful?

Here are my top VIP hacks and how to become more grateful instantly! Pick your favorites below and make sure you implement them on a daily basis.

1. When you wake up in the morning, go straight into speaking out loud what you're grateful for. Start listing them off. You could say something like 'I'm grateful for my strong healthy mind and body, I'm grateful for my bed, I'm grateful for the hot water in my shower, and I'm grateful for a new fresh start of the day!

2. Look back at your past and see what you have to be grateful for. Sometimes looking at the rearview mirror and conjuring up memories where you have experienced such an immense amount of gratitude can help you attract more blessings and set your mental tone for the day.

3. On your vision board, or your vision journal, take the time to post or write three things that make you happy and grateful.

4. Look at someone that is less fortunate than you. Think of someone who does not even have the everyday necessities that you take for granted.

Maybe hot running water, or even a toilet that flushes, or even nourishing food. When you see how they live, just give yourself the biggest and warmest hug and savor this moment knowing that you are highly positioned for unlimited potential.

5. Give! In order to feel like you automatically have more, give to someone who has less than you. Set up an automatic withdrawal from your bank account to give to a charity of your choice.

6. Faith it until you make it! Yes, you read this right! For instance, you want to have your dream job, dream salary, paid vacation, and a Christmas bonus check that would make your head spin. Faith it until you make it! Live as if you already have it. This is part of manifesting which is linked to being grateful. Be grateful that you already have it. When you act like you already have it through faith, you will actually manifest it, and manifest it faster.

<u>Fun-Work-What are you thankful for:</u>

_____

_____

_____

_____

_____

November

Happy NO-vember! Learning to Have Healthy Boundaries

> *"Lack of boundaries invites lack of respect, it's that simple. Boundaries define us. When we fail to set healthy boundaries we feel used and mistreated. So love yourself enough to set boundaries".-JNL*

Having boundaries doesn't mean being nasty and cruel. It's actually the opposite. It means that you care about others and yourself. You want to leave nothing to chance that feelings will get hurt, or people will feel used or taken advantage of.

Listen to Your Emotions

How do we know if our boundaries have been crossed? Your emotions are a very powerful indicator that either your loved ones, a business associate, or even an old friend have crossed your personal boundaries of comfort. If you feel used, if you feel taken advantage of, or if you feel misunderstood, or even at times some of your relationships feel one-sided, then most likely your boundaries have been crossed.

Why are Your Boundaries Crossed in the First Place?

Think about it? A very common reason why boundaries are crossed in the first place is that they were never clearly created, stated, and then reiterated. For instance, say you have a friend who likes to borrow your clothes, but never returns them, or she returns then in bad shape. Or this friend also calls you or texts you for every little thing, showing you disregard for your own personal time and space. It's possible that you have not created healthy boundaries in the first place. So, if you feel like this relationship is getting one-sided, and only helping her, and not helping you, you've not placed those boundaries in order from the get-go. Why? because you didn't even know what your boundaries were? As you evolve into a VIP woman, make sure you know what your boundaries are, by creating them, then stating them, and when people take advantage of you, you must be willing to reiterate them.

This leads me to a three-step VIP process of setting healthy boundaries.

The 3 Step VIP Process to Setting Healthy Boundaries

1. Create- First of all, you actually need to create your boundaries. Don't let people guess what your boundaries are. This holds true for your intimate relationships, business associates, even parent-child relationships. Anyone that you have a daily interaction with, you must set your healthy boundaries. Know exactly what you want, and be very crystal clear.

2. State- Now that you know what your boundaries are, please let everyone who plays a major role in your life know what your boundaries are. Yes, you heard me right! Take the time to state and share your boundaries with everyone. Invite them to do the same. Open communication that is honest and transparent is a healthy vehicle to create long-term wonderful relationships.

3. Reiterate- When you see others have not taken your boundaries seriously, put your foot down in a nice and courteous way. Kindly reiterate your boundaries, letting them know what you're willing to stand for. As you progress in your VIP power, this will become second nature to you. Again, it's not about being mean, it's about being nice and respectful to everyone in your life, including yourself.

Dysfunctional Passive-Aggressive Behavior, the Silent Treatment, and also Shutting Down

What happens if boundaries are not put in place? You will find very unhealthy broken-down relationships consisting of dysfunctional methods of communication such as passive aggressive behavior, the silent treatment, and also people just shutting down. We don't want that. We want to build healthy relationships that benefit both sides. So remember, in order to have functional relationships, and not fall into the trap of having dysfunctional, nonexistent or unhealthy communication, make it a point to create, state, and reiterate your boundaries.

FUN WORK: Write below how you plan on creating, stating and reiterating your boundaries:

_____

_____

_____

_____

_____

_____

_____

_____

_____

_____

_____

_____

_____

_____

_____

The VIP Power of Time Management: How to Reclaim and Own Your Time Again:

VIPS! I love this section of our VIP Power book! We are going to RECLAIM OUR TIME! We all have the same amount of time, but it's those who win at life who guard their time and who make the most out of every day! Have you ever had a long to-do list, but by the end of the day you barely scratched off two items? You may actually feel like a chicken with its head cut off, just running from task to task moving as best you could, but not getting anything done? Well those days are over! So let's focus on being productive and getting the results and desired outcomes that you want and deserve.

TIME IS MONEY

Time is money. You have heard this old adage for years. But it's true! Time is both valuable and limited, just like money! So, you must protect your time and make sure to budget it wisely.

Listen, I am not preaching to you. I am teaching you. I've been there, right where you are. I was one of the biggest time wasters ever! For half of my life, I didn't schedule my days and I was left to guessing. I wasted a lot of time. Shortly after the birth of my second son, I woke up and had my "A-ha" transformative moment in 2003. When I had my epiphany, I started to grab every second of my life, and make it work for the greater good for my loved ones, my family and me. When did you realize you had to stop wasting time? And start making time work for you?

Those who have great time-management skills are actually able to get their 4-6 VIP at-home workouts in per week. They are also able to get weekly grocery haul and their meal prep done. It's kind of cool to think about it this way: those who have good time management skills are also amazing athletes with their time. They are succinct, punctual, are in the moment, yet don't let events or tasks linger on, making sure they get to the point at hand, eloquently transitioning to the next

Make sure to get your work outs planned and also your highly nutritious meals prepped. It takes time to work out and prepare meals, therefore as your coach, I highly suggest that you put this in the forefront of your schedule.

The Power of 5 Minutes:

Yes, as your Coach, may I motivate you to measure our activities down to the nano-second! This transformation happened to me. I once thought 5 minutes is just 5 minutes, and I can't get a lot done in that measurement of time. Then I went to "I got 5 minutes, I can get a lot done in that time!" So I started setting the timer on my phone for 5 minutes, and I would for instance start cleaning the kitchen. This mind hack helped me to stop procrastination and get me up and going. And sometimes your task at hand will take longer than 5 minutes, but use this VIP tool to get the MOMENTUM going! So get your "shift" together, as in shifting your mindset. And let's make TIME WORK FOR YOU!

What made me change? I got sick and tired of not getting anything done by the end of the day. So I flipped it! I went from "going with the flow" to being "hyper-focused" on getting results.

Look at the lifestyle and wellness benefits that those with good time management techniques get to enjoy!

They:

- Feel less stressed

- Are more productive

- Get more things done more effectively

- Have more energy for things they need to accomplish

- Are able to do the things they want and relate more positively to others

- Feel better about themselves

- Feel more in control of their lives and future

Okay, you are sold! But your question is "Coach JNL, I know it's good to have solid time management skills, but HOW! Help me!"

Well, here comes the fun part!

We have all heard of to-do list. Well I want to flip it again and I want you to make a distraction list. Write down all the things that distract you that actually cause you to get less done

Distraction List:

_____

_____

_____

_____

_____

_____

_____

_____

_____

_____

_____

_____

_____

Okay here's more fun work! Take a look at the list above. Now completely take out all those distractions from your life. It's as simple as that!

Set Stern and Firm Deadlines: There is a powerful psychology to having deadlines. When you have a deadline, you will get it done. If you don't have a deadline, this allows you to not finish your tasks.

So the second step after you write your to-do list, is to write a deadline behind each task.

Prioritize Your Daily, Weekly, & Monthly Tasks: Set priorities to each task that you have to do for the day, the week, and the month. Focus on the bullseye. What is the most important task? What must get done first before you can complete the other ones? When you ask yourself very powerful questions as such, you get clear! So, break your to-do's down and tasks from top to bottom, focusing on the ones that are essential and of most importance and get those done first.

Plan Out Each Day and Then Visualize Going Through Every Step of Your Day: We've all heard of planning out each day ahead of time. But, we're missing the second step which is extremely vital. The second step is to actually visualize going through each step of your day. What I do before I even get out of bed is I imagine in my mind's eye what I'm going to do for the first 3 hours in my day. I actually physically see it play through my mind as I'm laying in bed before my feet hit the ground. This way, when I wake up I have a laser focus that nobody and nothing can penetrate or distract me from, I hit the floor running! So, next time before you get out of bed try this very powerful visualization exercise. See yourself taking the exact steps you need to take to get the most done for the next 3 hours. Remember, if you win the morning, you win the day!

Be Disciplined: You can have every appointment book, scheduling app, jumbo dry erase calendar, timers and beepers to time your tasks, but if you're not disciplined, none of that will matter. So, when you feel like you're slacking off, give yourself that much-needed motivational kick in the butt to get back up and on your winning VIP saddle. If you have to, go revisit your distraction list, and make sure you're not letting any of those activities flow back into your everyday lifestyle.

Multitask: In order to get more done in less time you have to learn how to multitask. Some other so-called experts and gurus say don't multitask. That's rubbish. As a mother of two boys, balancing home life, being a wife, career, and my fitness program, it was absolutely essential that I multi-task! It's like telling a short-order cook or a waitress that they need only focus on one thing at a time. That's a lie! If they did that they'd never be able to handle their shift, and they would be fired on the spot. Look, life is tough, you have a lot coming at you at all times. You need to learn how to get as much done as you can done in the little amount of time that we all have.

<u>Determine Your Productive Times:</u> Have you ever heard the saying, that we are smarter in the morning? Well, it's absolutely true. That's why the multi-millionaires of the world wake up at 5 a.m., extremely early every morning. They are able to get more done in that power hour when it's quiet, before the whole world wakes up, with less distraction, and a more rested mental state. You should try to do the same as it'll help you gain clarity as well. As the day drags on, your mental power, and ability to focus diminishes. So, grab the moments in the morning where you are the most refreshed and focused.

For example, if I have to ride out a class schedule I'm not going to do it last thing at night because it'll take me a full hour to get through it. Instead make sure you plan that in the early part of your day as I know personally it'll take me five minutes to complete it.

<u>Minimize interruptions and Remove Distractions:</u> It sounds so simple, yet it is extremely powerful: the more uninterrupted time you get during the day to work on important tasks, the more effective you'll be, and the more tasks you will accomplish. Identify the activities that tend to disrupt your work, and find a solution. Basically, one of the most essential_time management skills is to not get distracted. For example, don't check your emails or respond to text messages when you're in the middle of something important. Once you have broken your flow, it can be difficult to get back into it!

<u>Use a Timer</u>. The Power of Timers! This is probably one of my favorites time management hacks! This is such an easy VIP time management tool to implement tip. Say you have 6 tasks on your to-do list, but only 60 minutes to complete it all. Set a timer for 10 minutes and start on the most important task. Aim to finish before 10 minutes. Then start on the next, resetting the timer. If you go over 10 minutes, end that task where you left it. This is called "it's good enough" or also I like to say "it's as good as it's going to get" for right now. Continue to the next task. Follow through until one hour is up. And then just look at how much you have accomplished!

<u>Plan your work ahead</u> Let's go back to the section on how to win at life by looking at it as a chess game and always looking 10 steps ahead in advance pertaining to time management. Go ahead and capture the tasks and activities that you must do in the next 24 hours and update that list regularly during the day. Check back on your VIP power list occasionally and add new items as they appear, or cross off those that you have already completed. Make sure your list gives you a succinct overview of all that is important and urgent.

<u>Set Clear Priorities:</u> Clarity is key! If you don't know what your priorities are, you'll be all over the place wasting time and energy. So, be like a laser in the world of flashlights and focus on your top priorities.

<u>Stop Procrastinating</u>: One way to stop procrastinating goes back to giving yourself a strict deadline. So, if you have a hard time staying focused and tend to slack off and procrastinate, you'll be the one that will highly benefit from creating a deadline, or as I like to say an external commitment for yourself. For example, if you have 48 hours to get a project done, you have to make sure you will be done within 6 hours of that deadline. Always give yourself some elbow room for last-minute delays. I also love to tackle the most unpleasant parts of my to do list early in the day while my energy is fresh in order to allow myself the smaller rewards of knowing that I completed them! There's such a victorious feeling when I cross off the major mountains of tasks on my to-do list.

<u>Dry Erase Boards:</u> In order to stay focused throughout the day, and remain on task, I keep multiple dry erase boards around my desk. They allow me the freedom to jot down ideas and tasks as they come into my busy day. Ideas are like slippery fish and you have to grab them before they slip out of your hand. So if you jot them down on a dry erase board (or post it note, or iPad or cell phone note area, at least you have it recorded and you can look back at it to make sure you complete this task.)

<u>Learn to Delegate</u>: Not asking for help is a common trait in many people today. We have a hard time asking for help. We want to do it all ourselves. We must allow ourselves to be helped. Once we are able to request assistance, it'll lighten the load that we have to carry every

day. So, learning how to delegate is an essential part to the VIP skill set. Yes, a VIP woman is hardworking, and also ready, willing and able to have someone help her. I know in the past that I wanted to be Superwoman and do it all. But, I've learned how to delegate and it has really helped me move mountains. Even if it is just one person helping you, four hands work quicker than two. So, learn how to delegate and don't be afraid to ask for help.

Learn How to Say No: The word "NO" has immense power! It doesn't mean you're being rude, or being unkind. It actually means you're being upfront, honest and saving a lot of people time, energy and confusion. I have to say that this is the number one most powerful rule to time management. When you say no to a task or an activity that has nothing to do with your agenda, or tasks at hand, you actually are freeing up your schedule to be able to focus on what you need to focus on. So, start to say no to activities that have nothing to do with your goals. When you say yes and give your time, energy, and focus to activities that take away and distract you from your success plan, you are going to shine on your VIP throne. Now, don't get me wrong, I love doing charity work and helping out those less fortunate. I'm talking about giving your time and energy to that manipulative faux-friend, or toxic family member that only wants to drain you dry of every ounce of your focus and energy. Learn how to say no, and learn how to stick up for yourself, and don't look back!

<u>Summarize the Entire Day in the Morning:</u> The first time management skill of the day should be to determine what you actually want to achieve that day and what you absolutely must accomplish. Before you check your email or responding to text messages, become very clear on your intention for the day. Setting a clear focus for the entire day only requires as little as five minutes, but it can save you several hours of wasted time and effort.

<u>Set Your Intentions for the Day:</u> Here Comes divine intervention and your subconscious at work. We can have all the to-do lists and timers and strategic apps that help us stay focused on our tasks at hand. However if you set your intentions for the day at the beginning right when you wake up, you already subconsciously set yourself up to get more done with less effort. You see as your VIP success coach my goal is to help you naturally flow throughout the day getting more done, with less effort. So use my VIP tip of just sayingout loud and writing down your intentions for the day.

<u>Work Smarter, Not Harder:</u> When it comes to time management, it's all about working smarter not harder. In order to get max results in minimum time, you must see through the fluff, and cut to the chase. Just like a chess game, sometimes you have to take one step back to get 10 steps ahead.

<u>Measure Your Results, Not Your Time:</u> How do you stay motivated and feeling accomplished? Simple! You

measure your results, not your time! To be honest, sometimes we fool ourselves. Sometimes we sabotage ourselves from the start, because we feel like certain tasks should take us an hour to complete, but in all honesty, it could actually only take 10 minutes. So remember, keep moving, use your timers, and keep crossing off your items on your to-do list one by one! YES YOU CAN!

<u>Guard Your Time Like Millions of Dollars:</u> Let me ask you a question: if you had millions of dollars, would you put it in the bank? Guard it with your life? Or put it in a vault, and scrambled the lock? And not let anyone or anybody know your code? Exactly! You should do the same thing with your time! You are in control of your time! So, strategically use it. Guard it like millions of dollars. Don't let anybody or anything take your focus from you! Don't let anyone nickel-and-dime your time. Stay on top of your tasks and always be mindful of your time!

VIP Time Management Tip: To stop meetings running over, go ahead and let people know in advance what time you need to leave or even end the meeting even if you're having a business lunch date. Set yourself up for success from the start of the meeting and or lunch.

<u>Be Punctual!</u> If you are on time, you are Late: I always stress being on time. Let your friend or co-worker you are meeting with know that you have a tight schedule, and that your meeting needs to start on time, and what time

you have to leave. If they are 15-20 minutes late, and you have to go, leave. It's that simple. They need to get their "shift" together. And just because they don't have their shift together, this doesn't mean that you have to suffer.

It's Not a To Do List, It's an "Energy List": Don't Lose Sleep Over It! Say this powerful VIP mantra "I will sleep on it! I will have the answers in the morning!" Maintain your energy, as haste makes waste. Keep your vibration high, don't get flustered and focus on keeping your energy positive. Remember, negative vibes drains your energy, when positive vibes actually boosts your energy levels!

Fun Work: How do you plan on making your time work for you? What are your weak points for time management that you need to work on? How do you plan on making more time in your schedule? What are you going to say No to, in order to say YES to in your life?

_____

_____

_____

_____

_____

_____

_____

CHAPTER 12

DECEMBER: THE BIRTH OF JESUS CHRIST, SPIRITUALS LAWS OF SUCCESS, SEE YOUR VIP WELLNESS PROGRAM AS THE BEST GIFT YOU CAN GIVE YOURSELF THIS HOLIDAY SEASON, GIVE IN ORDER TO RECEIVE, THE LAW OF KARMA, AND A TIME OF REFLECTION & CELEBRATION!

*For unto us a child is born, to us a son is given,
and the government will be on his shoulders.
And he will be called Wonderful Counselor,
Mighty God, Everlasting Father, Prince of
Peace. -Isaiah 9:6*

December! The beautiful finale of this wonderful year! Take the time to look back at the past 11 months, give glory to God, and give yourself the biggest hug ever. You earned this moment. Not many made it this far. Many people mentally cracked under the pressure, they stressed themselves into sickness or they drove themselves mad mulling over negative situations that made them feel powerless and useless. But you on the other hand pushed through and not only survived, but you thrived! Congratulations!

December is one of my favorite months. Why? Well for many reasons. And, no, it's not because of all the Christmas gifts! It really is to celebrate first of all the birth of Jesus Christ. What a gift! I love the story of the wise men, how Jesus was born in a manger, and the North star. So many miracles!

This is the time where our hearts fill up with love, joy, and celebration with our friends and loved ones. In true VIP fashion, as I always say, giving is the new receiving, I love to give gifts and to see the joy on my loved ones faces.

This brings me to one of my personal favorite spiritual laws, The Law of Giving. You must give in order to receive.

But this is just one spiritual law of many! And since this is such a spiritual time, a time for rebirth, renewal, celebrating miracles, and a time to believe, and have more faith, I like to take the time to cover the seven spiritual laws of success. As you read over them, pick your favorite one. Also pick the one that you're really strong in. Also pick the one that you need to work on more. Let's do this!

The Seven Spiritual Laws of Success

1. The **Law** of Pure Potentiality. The source of all creation is pure consciousness.

2. The **Law** of Giving. The universe operates through dynamic exchange.

3. The **Law** of "Karma" or Cause and Effect.

4. The **Law** of Least Effort.

5. The **Law** of Intention and Desire.

6. The **Law** of Detachment

7. The **law** of "Dharma" or Purpose In Life.

Now that we know the seven Spiritual Laws of Success, let's go one by one into a little bit more detail.

The Law of Pure Potentiality

The source of all creation is pure consciousness. It is pure potentiality seeking expression from the unmanifest to the manifest. When we realize that our true self is one of pure potentiality, we align with the power that manifests everything in the universe.

The Law of Giving

The universe operates through dynamic exchange. Giving and receiving are different aspects of the flow of energy in the Universe. In our willingness to give that which we seek, we keep the abundance of the universe circulating in our lives.

The Law of "Karma" or Cause and Effect

Every action generates a force of energy that returns to us in like kind. What we sow is what we reap. When we choose actions that bring happiness and success to others, the fruit of our karma is happiness and success.

The Law of Least Effort

Nature's intelligence functions with effortless ease, freeness, harmony, and love. When we harness the forces of harmony, joy, and love, we create success and good fortune with effortless ease.

The Law of Intention and Desire

Inherent in every intention and desire is the mechanics for its fulfillment. Intention and desire in the field of pure potentiality have infinite organizing power. When we introduce an intention in the fertile ground of pure potentiality, we put this infinite organizing power to work for us.

The Law of Detachment

In detachment lies the wisdom of uncertainty in the wisdom of uncertainty lies the freedom from our past, from the known, which is the prison of past conditioning. In our willingness to step into the unknown, the field of all possibilities, we surrender ourselves to the creative mind that orchestrates the dance of the universe.

The law of "Dharma" or Purpose In Life

Everyone has a purpose in life, a unique gift or special talent to give to others. When we blend this unique talent with service to others, we experience the ecstasy and exultation of our own spirit, which is the ultimate goal of all goals.

See Your VIP Wellness Program as the Best Gift You Can Give Yourself this Holiday Season,

As we get caught up in the hustle and bustle of the hectic holiday season, let us not forget the greatest gift we can give ourselves - the gift of exercise and our VIP wellness program. The www.JNLVIP.com wellness program is the gift that keeps on giving! So, as we are buying gifts, wrapping presents, and boxing up surprises for other people that are on our holiday list, don't forget to make sure you put yourself on your gift-giving list. Continue to give yourself the gift of exercise.

Remember in the previous chapters I talked about how we are susceptible to gaining a lot of weight during the high calorie stressful holiday season. Don't let this happen to you. Don't let all of your hard work that you focused on this entire year to go to waste in just four weeks. Make working out fun during the holiday season. You can do holiday themed workouts and don't forget your fun Santa hat!

Keep it lean clean and green! Enjoy peppermint protein shakes, or remake your Christmas classic recipes as a healthier version. This is the time to celebrate your VIP cheer with all your loved ones near and far.

Time of Reflection

One thing we do too little of is reflect. Take this time to reflect on the past 11 months of this beautiful year. How did you get stronger? How did you get healthier? Look how far you have come! You should have an overwhelming sense of pride, accomplishment, and joy. Reflective thinking helps us plan and it also gives insight. Reflection is a process of exploring and examining ourselves, our perspectives, attributes, experiences and actions / interactions. It helps us gain insight and see how to move forward. Reflection is often done as writing, meditating, thinking, or just spending quiet time reminiscing about your favorite memories in the past year, or even the hardest, most challenging times and how you got through them. Allow yourself to enjoy looking back! When you do, you allow yourself the opportunity to see just how amazing you are!

VIP Key to Success: Start Writing Your Life's Success Story by Writing Your Last Chapter:

It's December. The last month of the year. Think about this entire year as a book, with 12 Chapters. The last Chapter, you should "write first". At the beginning of January, I always ask my clients where they want to be by the end of the year. I make sure they visualize what goals they want to accomplish. Maybe they want to own a home. Maybe they want to finally release that project they've been working on. Whatever it is, I make sure they see it in high definition, crystal clear! This is the magic! You have to look again just like a chess game, can you see what your goals are? You must have clarity so that from there you can reverse engineer and manifest the vision that you hold. So, always start with your end goal in mind.

For instance, next month in January we will actually then ask ourselves, "Where do we want to be in December? What goals must we meet? Then you reverse your plan of attack from December, to November, it's October and so forth. This way we can set short-term and long-term goals.

So in conclusion, a VIP woman knows what she wants. She has removed all blocks. She has let go of all silent counter intentions. She's done the inner work and now she's ready to create and enjoy the outer work! A major VIP key to success is knowing what you want your last chapter of your life to look like. That should be your bullseye. And always keep your eye on the prize. So when you are writing your book on your life, Always start with the last chapter! Then reverse-engineer. Rewind the steps you need to make in order to get there. It'll give you tons of crystal clear clarity if you attack your goals this way.

Since this month is very spiritual for all of us as we get to celebrate our higher power and truly give thanks for all the miracles, I would like to share one of my favorite prayers. It is called the Serenity Prayer.

The Serenity Prayer is a prayer written by the American theologian Reinhold Niebuhr. It is commonly quoted as:

God, grant me the serenity to accept the things I cannot change, courage to change the things I can, and wisdom to know the difference.

This is such a powerful prayer! It touches upon the notion that we should not waste. Therefore to save your time and energy focusing on things that you can change, and also the intelligence to know the difference. I pray that this month we will remind ourselves to pick our battles and that we understand the concept that sometimes we have to "lose in order to win."

Let's Celebrate

5, 4, 3, 2, 1, HAPPY NEW YEAR! I love this time of year where we close at one year and ring in the middle! Let us start this New Year with the intention of creating more magic, miracles, and success breakthroughs! Now, here's my coaching advice to you, don't let all your hard work this past year slip through your fingers by allowing yourself to slide back to any negative habits. Keep your eye on the prize! Be resilient! Be persistent! Keep building on the success that you created last year. Embrace the new year with new energy and a fresh perspective on all the possibilities of a new you. May it catapult all of your goals straight into the next stratosphere of success!   Okay new year, LETS DO THIS!

Use this space below to jot down any notes you like to capture for the new year. And remember, this is not the end of the book, this is just the beginning of the journey! If you're not a VIP member, continue your wellness journey and rock the virtual red carpet every day of your life by joining www.JNLVIP.com You will lock in your success, get the support you need, get direct access to me, your helpful and loving coach, as well as joining a non-judgmental super positive group of women on a global level who are ready, willing, and able to cheer for you and root you on!

NOTES FOR CHAPTER 12:

_____

_____

_____

_____

_____

_____

_____

_____

_____

_____

_____

_____

_____

_____

_____

HOW TO WIN THE WAR ON ANXIETY, DEPRESSION, WORRY AND DOUBT.

I made a last minute decision to add this as an entire chapter by itself because anxiety, depression, worry, and doubt were recurring spiritual challenges that kept on popping up when I was either coaching my clients, or listening to my VIPs in our private "faith-book" group.

I got sick and tired of hearing that women were prescribed medication only to make their problems worse, and also then forcing them to gain weight, get tired, and suffer from chronic fatigue. I saw many women waste months, if not years, trying to fight and win the war against anxiety and panic attacks when nothing seemed to help. I am not against medication. There's a time and place for everything. What I am for is exhausting all measures possible in order for us as human beings to finally get control over our brain, our emotions, and our bodies so we can obtain true self-mastery, instead of us being a slave to our mind, body, and emotions.

I guess I took for granted that I healed myself from anxiety. Yes, I'm not lying. I healed myself. I had no choice. It was either I die of anxiety, or I find a way to survive and create mind hacks that work.

My personal story of anxiety & how I "healed" myself

My personal story of anxiety is quite frankly exceptional. Not to drag it out, or go into too many details, I had a horrific childhood. It wasn't the basic "I don't feel loved" kind of childhood. It was a childhood where I was not taken care of, my mom and dad were pretty much negligent parents. I didn't have the basic necessities. I lived on the poverty level, and to put it lightly, I suffered immense emotional abuse. I'm not having a pity party, I just want to let you know the extent of the bleakness of my earliest days that I can remember.

Think about it, when you are a child, and you don't have anyone to turn to, you are going to suffer.

Therefore, needless to say, I had many episodes of anxiety, panic attacks, worry, doubt, and just basically living in fear.

Fast forward to my early teenage years. I started to figure out that it was up to me in order to make sense of all this craziness. So I did. I actually requested my mother to take me to counseling which we did, only to have the counselor tell my mom that she was the one that needed to get professional help, and not me. I breathed a sigh of relief. I knew I wasn't crazy and I knew I had my head on straight. I knew I just had a rough childhood but I could get through it.

And I did get through it. How? Easy! I followed these basic steps which helped me crack the code on my own anxiety, and I didn't have to take any prescription medicine.

1. Acceptance

2. Inner Strength

3. Faith

4. Believe in a higher power

5. Believing in karma

6. Perseverance

7. Never playing the victim

8. Taking 100% responsibility for my own outcomes

9. Never blaming anyone

10. Staying above the fray

11. Actually taking myself to the point of having anxiety to see if I could manage my emotions.

12. Working out

13. Eating lean clean and green, high vibrational Whole Foods

14. Getting off all stimulants

15. No Pulling All Nighters

16. Little to no caffeine

17. Vitamins

18. Sun, Outdoors

19. Adequate rest

20. Guided meditation

21. Aroma aromatherapy

22. Talking it out with myself

23. Journaling

24. Gratitude

25. Being not paranoid, but the opposite, Pronoia

26. I've learned to not put myself in stressful situations that would trigger anxiety

27. I would say what is the worst that could happen. And accept it. And be at peace with it.

28. I learned to grow through what I go through.

29. I learned to find calmness in the chaos.

30. To Never Live in Regret. Just to Live & Learn.

Now those are my top 30 lifestyle hacks to heal anxiety. Let's go through them one by one to dig a little bit deeper.

1. Acceptance: Once you accept a certain situation in your life, your brain automatically clicks into the positive mode of "okay, I got this, it is what it is, I will get stronger through this!" As the saying goes, what doesn't kill you only makes you stronger! Having this type of mindset will be very productive and helpful for you to keep on kicking butt and never giving up.

2. Inner Strength: One of the greatest gifts that I received from suffering through anxiety is the ability to summon the inner strength to come out unscathed. So, if you are still experiencing anxiety or panic attacks, just know if you made it through one episode, you can make it through a thousand more. Once you accept that, going back to point number one, you pretty much have squashed the fear of having anxiety or panic attacks.

3. Faith: Through the hard times of anxiety, panic attack, worry, doubt, confusion, this is where your faith is born. Or as I like to say, "Faith-it Till You Make It!" Use your faith! No matter how little your faith is, once you know that you can and will make it through any future anxiety, panic attacks, worry, doubt, or depression, you have won the inner battle, and now you can win the outer battle.

4. Believe in a Higher Power: During my anxiety episodes, I always knew that there was a higher power watching over me. It is as if I was going through mental training Boot Camp only to get tougher and stronger with every strike that was put against me. I knew that I wasn't alone. I leaned into my higher power, during my darkest times. It was as If I knew if I could just make it through one more day that the days would get easier, one day at a time.

5. Believe in karma: A lot of the time, my anxiety, depression, doubt, or worry was triggered from people doing me wrong or unfair situations. Instead of exhausting myself and trying to " dance with the devil' and fighting back or trying to get even, I just let it go. I knew that karma, one of the most powerful spiritual laws of the universe, would take care of all the dirty work. This freed up my mental space. You receive a great sense of inner peace when you know you do not need to go and get even. Don't waste your time, energy or focus on lowering your vibration to get even with someone else who did you wrong. You are just adding fuel to the fire. You're only going to increase your anxiety because you won't feel good about yourself if you reacted in a negative way. Get out of the way. Let go and let God.

6. Perseverance: every episode of anxiety that I was able to manage, and come out of unharmed, proved to me that I had the perseverance, the intestinal fortitude, the indomitable will, mental strength, and emotional fortitude to make it through.

7. I never played the victim. Some people who take on the role of victim might seem to enjoy blaming others for problems that they cause; lashing out and making others feel guilty, or manipulating others for sympathy and attention. This is also associated with narcissistic personality disorder. Don't be this type of person.

8. Taking 100% responsibility for my own outcomes- it is you and only you that's responsible for your outcomes.

9. Never blaming anyone - Once we stop playing the blame game, we can get the clear picture and a firm handle on the situation of anxiety.

10. Stay Above the Fray-Don't get dragged into unnecessary fights from hostile people, toxic family members, or people out to ruffle your feathers. That can evoke a whole slew of negative emotions including anxiety, stress, and depression.

11. Actually taking myself to the point of having anxiety to see if I could manage my emotions. Yes

it's true, time and time again when I had anxiety, I literally was getting tougher every time to see how much I could handle and how strong my emotions were. So, every about anxiety attack that you have, just know that it's only making me stronger.

12. Working out- yes we all know the power of a good workout! When you release all of the positive "good feeling" neurotransmitters such as dopamine, anxiety doesn't stand a chance.

13. Eating lean clean and green, high vibrational whole foods- you cannot have a clear head when you're on the cigarette and Red Bull energy drink diet. We see how people get extremely mentally ill overnight when they don't eat healthy. Remember you are what you eat! The food you eat affects your mind, body and spirit. So fuel up on Mother Nature's goodness and eat whole foods.

14. Getting off all stimulants-Get off the uppers and the downers. Get off all medications if you can. Especially alcohol as it is a depressant.

15. No Pulling All Nighters - Good old-fashioned solid beauty sleep always supports a strong mental state.

16. Little to no caffeine- Going back to getting off all stimulants, obsessive use of caffeine is not good

for the mental state. Maybe a cup at most 2 in the morning if anything. It can cause Jitters, nervousness, which then evokes anxiety.

17. Vitamins- Make sure you give your body what it needs by enjoying a multivitamin

18. Sun and the Outdoors – There's nothing like feeling the warm sun on your skin! It can definitely brighten your mood! Getting in touch with nature can definitely make you feel more balanced and grounded.

19. Adequate rest - In addition to a solid night's rest, make sure you also work in any needed meditations during the day or power catnaps.

20. Guided Meditation- These are powerful tools that you can listen to with your eyes closed that can help you gain your composure and a greater sense of inner happiness.

21. Aromatherapy- Many people find that aromatherapy with certain essential oils can help promote relaxation and relieve stress and anxiety.

22. Talking it out- Just the simple act of talking it out, either with someone or even yourself will help you to reclaim your composure and let go of any anxiety, stress, depression or doubt.

23. Journaling - This is a powerful exercise that can aid in giving you clarity and foresight.

24. Gratitude- When you're grateful it's impossible to feel anxious.

25. Don't Be Paranoid, but Be the Opposite, Pronoiad! instead of thinking the entire universe is against you, flip it and think the exact opposite, that the universe is always working in your best interest and he's on your side.

26. I've learned to not put myself in stressful situations that would trigger anxiety - never put yourself in a situation where you won't win. I look back at some of the decisions that I've made. I was literally the one that was at fault for putting myself in a situation where I could only fail. So, make sure you don't set yourself up for failure but set yourself up for success.

27. I would say to myself, "what is the worst that could happen", and then accept it. The outcome was being at peace with the situation, and myself.

28. I learned to grow through what I go through - remember the universe brings you gifts every day, they're called experiences, both good and bad. It's up to us to grow through what we go through. Accept the life lessons, and move powerfully through life with your VIP power.

29. I learned to find calmness in the chaos - Look, life is like a big hurricane with winds that can get really big, and also eventually waiver, giving you

a break. I've learned to have tranquil moments even in times of trials and tribulations. It just takes extreme mental strength and focus, but the more you do it, the easier it gets.

30. To Never Live in Regret. Just to Live & Learn. At the end of the day we must look back at our lives and say, I lived to the fullest, and I regret nothing. The key is to simply live and learn. That's the great thing about life, that we get to live and learn and move on.

We are Wired to Have Anxiety, So Accept It As Being "Normal"

When you accept having anxiety, and see it as being normal, it diminishes its power. Know that we're all going to have some type of uncontrollable nerves, and that we're able to tame and gain control of. It's when we perceive these emotions to be abnormal that gives them the capacity to spiral out of control.

Why do our brains seem obsessed with problems, both real and imagined?

It's your default setting, so it's not your fault that we suffer from anxiety and that our brains are obsessed with problems both real and fake.

Let's get off the "Worry-Go-Round"! I'm here to help you finally realize that actually your brain is programmed and wired to believe that danger is around every corner. This is because an old trait in our wiring that helped ancient humans to live another day. Obviously that wiring is obsolete. It doesn't help us. It just makes us sick. Even at night when we lie awake, we may find ourselves up at night obsessing over fears of being sick, the death of loved ones, financial crisis, accidents and anything else that our brains tell us is a potential threat.

How do you stop worrying? You have to flood your brain daily with dopamine, oxytocin and serotonin, the good feeling neurotransmitters. How do you do this? Easily! By exercising, and linking pleasure to positive movement, eating as healthy as you can, and getting your adequate rest. Remember your brain is a 24-hour pharmacy giving you all that you need to feel good at any given moment! As a VIP woman we know how to tap into this!

Being Anxious is "Good"- Well, let me explain! If you remember that being anxious is actually part of how your brain is wired, and it is good for you because it helps you stay out of danger, this will help you to relax more and be able to get control of your anxiety.

Fight or Flight-We've all heard of the two responses that are triggered when we are in danger. We either fight, or flight, meaning run away. Well I didn't like any of those two. Fighting only would exhaust me, and running away meant that the problem was still there. So, I created a third response of my own and it is to make friends with it, embrace it, absorb it, and take in the energy and flip it back on the situation. Almost like a stealth ninja Jedi Master move, where you transform the negative energy of the moment into a positive one.

Think: What is the Worst That Can Possibly Happen & Accept the Worst Outcome.

What's the remedy to a cold? Taking cough syrup every 6 hours, rest, and some chicken noodle soup. So what's the remedy to anxiety? Taking the time to deliberate "what's the worst that can happen", and then accepting this worst case scenario. Try the following technique when you face anxiety, fear, nervousness, or worry: See in your mind's eye all possible negative consequences of the situation you are confronting. If you can learn how to alter your emotional landscape, then your brain will learn how to rewire itself.

It boils down to this, to get rid of anxiety you must first embrace it. When you do this powerful exercise, it's plain to see just how worked up we get about the smallest situation. When you envision the worst case scenario, and accept it, it isn't that bad. We can then look back objectively and see we truly have nothing to worry about.

Nervous About a Certain Situation? Play it Through Your Head Beforehand

The power of visualization is so useful that gold medal Olympic athletes use this technique in order to give it for the toughest of competitions. NASA astronauts use visualization before their walks on the moon. If it's good enough for gold medal athletes, as well as NASA astronauts, it's good enough for me! I use this technique when I was nervous about a certain situation. I would play it through my head beforehand multiple times before the actual event happened. This way, you familiarize yourself with these events, making them so common that you don't get bothered by it or nervous when the real event happens.

Exercise - This is your VIP weapon on fighting anxiety, stress, depression, worry, and doubt. You must bathe their brain in the trilogy of the most powerful neurotransmitters serotonin, dopamine, and oxytocin.

Meditate- When we meditate, we diminish the effects of anxiety. It's as simple as that. Meditation, which is the practice of focused concentration, bringing yourself back to the moment over and over again, actually reduces stress. Meditation is so powerful that not only can it help anxiety, it can also reduce the areas of chronic pain, depression, heart disease and high blood pressure. So, make sure you schedule in 10-15 minutes of meditation every day!

<u>Journal</u>-this is a very therapeutic and easy to implement exercise that will reduce stress that could eventually trigger anxiety. Journal your emotions. Transcribe how you feel. Record important data so that you can look back and reflect to see what causes you to go into a downward spiral of negative emotion.

<u>Pray</u> - When you pray it's like the hotline to your higher power and when you meditate and get those internal nuggets, it's God speaking back to you. This will help diminish anxiety and worry and doubt and replace it with faith, confidence, and inner peace.

So, there you have it! As you can see we're all wired to have anxiety. It was a built in mechanism to actually HELP us, not HURT us! So, don't overthink it. I think a lot of times we add gasoline to the fire when we stress over having anxiety. Once we understand that it's a temporary state of mind, and we learn how to get control over emotions, we gain power over fear in our lives.

NOTES:

_____

_____

_____

_____

_____

_____

_____

_____

_____

_____

_____

_____

_____

_____

_____

_____

_____

BONUS CHAPTER

THE "UN-DIET" DIET!
THE VIP FUN FIT FOODIE

Lean Clean and Green Approach to Eating!

Welcome to an extremely important section that will help you crack your fat loss code through the power superfoods! Many of you remember and also have my Fun Fit Foodie Cookbook. Think of this section as an extension of that book. Let's continue to celebrate your fun fit foodie spirit!

History: I am grateful to have close to 20 years of experience as a specialist in Sports Nutrition, supplementation, and helping my clients learn to love healthy food again. I've seen all crazy types of fad diets from what bikini competitors do, to those that want to drop some serious weight fast. I've been horrified at the drastic measures people do to lose weight, in extreme unhealthy ways. From crash dieting, which only kills your metabolism to eating little to nothing and exercising 3 hours a day. I'm here to put an end to all of this! This is why I coined the phrases "The Fun Fit Foodie" and "Lean Clean and Green".

The Fun Fit Foodie brand embodies the joyous spirit of making eating healthy food fun again! You see, I hate the word diet! What are the first three letters of the word diet? DIE! And that's exactly what we don't want to do!

The phrases "lean clean and green" really simplifies the entire notion of eating healthy. Make sure that your food choices are clean, meaning no unnecessary salt, sodium, as organic as possible, and no added preservatives. The word green represents fresh organic vegetables and fruits that puts an emphasis on having more of a plant-based focused meal plan.

If Man Made It, Don't Eat It: A cornerstone of the undiet diet is that if man made it don't eat it. Try to eat as close to mother nature as possible, meaning whole foods. Foods in their original form, taken straight from earth.

Why Diets Don't Work: There are many reasons why diets don't work. First of all, the diets are so overly confusing, and extremely difficult to follow. It is an unsustainable way of living. It's like being chained and imprisoned to a way of eating. There's no freedom in dieting. I know because I've been there. It was the most horrible experience ever having to look at a piece of paper and see what do I eat now? Or asking myself, if I can have this certain food combined with another food. Or even being deprived of eating healthy fruits which are high in nutrients and vitamins, just because they have a little sugar. Let me dive deeper. When someone hands you a diet, they're actually setting you up for failure. You must re-train your mind gut connection, your mouth-to-stomach connection, and also really listen to your satiation levels. Having someone hand you a piece of paper with a diet on it puts all of that personalized intuition to the side. This is extremely detrimental to your lifelong well-being.

The Fun Fit Foodie Lean Clean & Green Meal Formula:

> LEAN SOURCE OF PROTEIN + ½ CUP OF COMPLEX CARBS + ½ CUP OF FIBROUS CARB (VEGETABLE/SALAD) TABLESPOON OF HEALTHY FAT

Very simple. I highly suggest that you train first thing in the morning because this will boost your metabolism. For max fat blasting results, aim to work out on an empty stomach, so you can burn stored fat. Then within the first 60 minutes after your workout, enjoy a post workout meal complete with a lean source of protein, slow burning carb, and healthy fat. Again, even if you're not hungry, you have to eat within 1 hour after workout not to "lose your gains". Why? Because you will not be giving your body what it needs in order to repair muscle, and recover from the workout, and even slowing down your metabolism. Your body may very well go into starvation mode.

Then enjoy a lunch with a half a cup of complex carbs, and make sure you get a tablespoon of healthy fat.

Make sure you eat in the late afternoon around 3 or 4, and that should be your last complete carb of the day. This will be a small snack to hold you over till dinner.

Dinner is the exact meal formula, but without the complex carb. So you have a lean source of protein with half a cup of fibrous carb which is a vegetable. For instance a salad or a steamed veggie.

I do like fruit, but I highly suggest that you have it with your post workout meal or lunch. And to have your fruit early on in the day because it does contain sugar and we want to keep as many carbs in your food plan before 4.

Why The Fun Fit Foodie Lean Clean and Green Diet Works!

The Fun Fit Foodie Lean Clean and Green approach to eating works for many reasons. First of all it works with the metabolism not against it.

We focus on super foods that are high in antioxidants to help you "age in reverse" and fight off disease.

The VIP Rule of thumb is to eat breakfast like a queen, lunch like a princess, & dinner like a pheasant, trickling down your calories from the beginning of the day to the end. .

<u>Portion Distortion:</u> we live in a world of super-size and biggie size, and it is hard not to suffer from "portion distortion". This is where the #LCG magic comes into play. Once you are able to look at a piece of food and "size it up" with your eyes, you won't have to rely on the measuring cups so much.

To Count Macros or Not? That is the Question?

If counting macros works for you, great! If it's too confusing and time-consuming, I highly suggest that you don't. A general rule of thumb that will set you up for long-term success is to actually go back to portion control and also the "Fun Fit Foodie" formula. This will keep you within the guidelines, and also help save your sanity! Plus it is so hard to pinpoint how many macros you need because we are all different ages, with different DNA make up, varying genetics and we all have different levels of healthy metabolism.

Does Counting Calories Work?

This is a great question - yes it does help. But will it help you lose weight? Not necessarily. You can count all the calories in the world, and actually stay in your caloric count, but still gain weight or not even lose a pound. Why? I cover this topic in the metabolism section below.

Eating Instinctually, Listening to Your Gut

Respect Your Hunger Signals: Enjoy adequate energy and carbohydrates to keep your body biologically fed, or you can create a primitive drive to overeat. You must rebuild trust in yourself and in making healthy food decisions.

Say No to the Old Outdated "Diet" Mentality: Toss the diet mags and books that give you false hope of the quick fix! I Quite frankly got angry and set up with the entire Fitness industry that promote weight loss lies that actually led me to feel like a failure every time! Not only did I starve myself, but I killed my metabolism, and caused metabolic damage. I lost the weight quickly, but I gained it back faster plus more! This is why I totally love intuitive eating and listening to my mind body connection.

Listen To your Cravings and Make Peace with Food: When you listen to your cravings, and enjoy a little bit of what you are yearning for, you actually have control of the situation. The more you fight and suppress it, the stronger those cravings will build up. leading you to cave in to your forbidden foods. As the saying goes, what you resist persists! And then you're going to overeat with such intensity which can lead to overwhelming guilt.

Be Satisfied: In our quest to comply with the extreme diet culture, sadly enough we often dismiss one of the most fundamental gifts of life, which is a pleasure that can be found in eating. Look, I'm Italian! We love to eat! I knew that I had to create a sustainable food plan and it allowed me to enjoy myself, and never feel guilty because I was eating it. The Asians have it down to a science. They practice keeping food as one of their healthy living pleasures, allowing them to eat what they really want, in an environment that is warm, inviting, and the happiness you will enjoy will be such a powerful experience and helping you to feel content and satisfied. When you eat in this enjoyable experience, you will find that it takes just the right amount of healthy food for you to make the decision that you are "full".

This leads me to the next point!

Healthy Fats are Essential to "Be Full"

We've all tried the low-fat to fat-free diet. It made us feel exhausted, with thin hair, and also endless cravings. Why? Because your body actually needs essential fats. So in order to eat like a VIP, make sure you get your healthy serving of fats, from nuts, seeds, olive oil, coconut oil, MCT Oil, avocados and healthy fats! Monounsaturated fats and polyunsaturated fats are known as the "good fats" because they are good for your heart, your cholesterol, and your overall health. These fats can help to lower the risk of heart disease and stroke. Lower bad LDL cholesterol levels, while increasing good HDL.

And yes, these fats will help you to feel fuller faster, and also satiated for hours.

So to honor your fullness, you need to trust that you will give yourself the foods that you desire. Listen for the body signals that tell you that you are no longer hungry. Observe the signs that show that you're comfortably full. I usually like to drink a glass of water before I eat, and also drink lots of water during my meal to help me feel satiated quicker.

<u>VIP LEAN CLEAN AND GREEN TIP:</u> Pause in the middle of eating and ask yourself how the food tastes, and what your current hunger level is. Taking this time to reflect will help you gauge on how much you need to eat for the remainder of your meal. Even if you have a lot of food on your plate, please stop well before you are full. A Scale 1-10 you should ideally stop eating at a 7 or 8 because it takes your mind to catch up with your stomach fullness.

<u>Mindful VIP Movement:</u> Shift your focus from working out to burn calories to actually feeling how good it is to move your body, and to enjoy the dopamine, serotonin, and oxytocin that are released during the workout.

Forget exercise to lose weight! Just get active and *feel* the difference. Shift your focus to how it feels so good to move your body, rather than just focusing on the calorie-burning effect of exercise. If you focus on how incredible and powerful feelings you get from working out, it can make the difference between rolling out of bed for a VIP workout or hitting the snooze button!

Your Metabolism: Is it One Match? Or a Roaring Bon-fire?

Sadly enough, a lot of us have a broken metabolism. Metabolic damage is like a broken thermostat to your body's ability to burn fat. A sign of a broken metabolism is when your weight is stuck no matter how much exercise or dieting you do. I'm here to help you give some top tips on how to repair a broken metabolism.

- Make sure you get 8 hours of high-quality sleep per night

- Eat probiotic rich foods or take probiotic supplements

- Meditate daily to keep stress to a minimum.

- Get at least 4 to 6 metabolism boosting workouts in a week, like our VIP work out method

Hacks:

Enjoy a ½ to 1 tablespoon MCT OIL! Kiss My Keto is a high quality brand, and you can use code JNL for a VIP discount

Drink tons of lemon water

Make sure you choose our VIP Workouts over steady state cardio for max fat and calorie burn

Fitness Snacks. Enjoying a 5 to 15 minute mini workout to give yourself a fresh jolt of energy.

Drink Kombucha: its full of healthy probiotic bacteria and is believed to improve digestion and immune function. Because drinking kombucha likely aids in digestion, it must help improve metabolism —the process by which your body turns food into energy

Why Your Weekly Food Hauls are Fun, Essential and Important!

We all heard the saying "out of sight, out of mind". Well, let's flip it. "Insight, in mind". Place healthy food options right in the forefront, such as a bowl of unsalted nuts, fresh fruits and vegetables. How do you do this on a Consistent basis? Make your weekly food halls fun as they are essential and important! Choose one day out of the week that works best for your schedule. Me and my VIP clients around the world have selected Sunday as it's a day of rest and you have more time to do your grocery shopping and prep your meals for the week.

I can tell you that if you fail to prepare, just prepare to fail. From my countless coaching consultations I have learned that one of the major downfalls that sabotages many of my clients, is failing to do your weekly food haul.

We end up eating accidentally, going through the drive-thru, eating at the vending machine, or grabbing whatever food we can find last minute because we did not take the time to do our grocery shopping for the week.

Link pleasure to gathering your fun fit foodie lean clean and green goodies for the week. I pretend I'm a farm or actually going to my garden when I go to the grocery store. I'm picking up fresh produce I know will nourish my body and my soul. Whatever kind of mind hack you have to do to get yourself to the grocery store, or have your healthy produce delivered, do it! Something that is so basic that we kind of take for granted is actually one of the most important steps to cracking your VIP fat loss code.

Can't Stop Eating it? Don't Bring it Into the House

Client: "Help coach JNL! I can't stop eating Oreos and Twinkies!"

Me: "Well who's bringing it into the house?"

Client: "Me"

Can you see how ludicrous this conversation is? If you can't stop eating it, don't bring it in the house! You're setting yourself up for failure.

Healthy Swap Solution

Instead, replace your desire for chips and crackers with crunchy chopped up vegetables.

If you're craving ice cream, swap it out for fat-free Greek yogurt topped with fresh berries.

Still craving Oreos? Swap it out for cookies and cream inspired protein bar.

You can swap any unhealthy food with a healthy life! It's as simple as that!

How to Stop Emotional Eating

I'm really excited about this section! Why? Because it has been proven that most women sabotage their fat loss success because they are triggered to emotionally eat. So we are going to finally once and for all get a handle on our emotional eating and understand that \ diving into a big bowl of macaroni and cheese does not fix any of our problems, it only makes it worse! Let's do this!

Are You an Emotional Eater? To find out if you are an emotional eater, answer yes or no to the questions below.

1. Do you eat more when you're feeling stressed?

2. Do you eat when you're not hungry or when you're full?

3. Do you eat to feel better, such as to calm and soothe yourself when you're sad, mad, bored, anxious?

4. Do you reward yourself with food?

5. Do you regularly eat until you've stuffed yourself?

6. Does food make you feel safe? Do you feel like food is a friend?

7. Do you feel powerless or out of control around food?

Food does not fix "emotional hunger". Even though Your brain believes that by eating you are fixing your emotions, this is a lie, and usually you often feel horrible because of the unnecessary calories you just scarfed down. Then you beat yourself up for not having power over your mouth emotions, and little to no willpower.

Then, the problem only deepens. You can feel powerless over food and then your feelings. Well, I'm here to give you some hope! Yes, you can learn healthier ways to crush your cravings, have a healthy relationship with triggering better emotions, and setting yourself up for Success. Let's finally take off the hand-cuffs of emotional eating!

Differentiate Between Physical Hunger and Emotional Hunger

If you regularly use food to deal with your feelings, we must learn how to distinguish between emotional and physical hunger.

Since emotional hunger can be powerful, it's easy to confuse it for physical hunger. But, there are red flags that help you decipher emotional hunger apart from physical hunger.

Feelings Trigger Emotional Hunger Fast: Emotional hunger hits you like a ton of bricks. It comes in Fast & Furious. On the other hand, physical hunger comes on more naturally and gradually. The urge to eat doesn't feel as life-or-death, like a demand for instantaneous satisfaction.

Comfort Foods are the Crutch for Emotional Hunger

Junk food, high carb foods, sugary treats give you that instant rush that is triggered by emotions. This is emotional hunger. But when you're physically hungry, healthy options like salads, grilled vegetables, and detox soups sound delicious! When you're emotionally hungry, you need to eat a certain food and nothing else will be able to take its place.

Mindless Eating is Emotional Eating:

When you eat mindlessly, it's like you're eating in a Time lapsed tunnel, before you know it, you down two whole bag of Doritos or a tub of ice cream. You can eat an entire Pizza without really paying attention or fully enjoying it. You look back and think, wow I just ate that? But, when you're eating it in response to physical hunger you're more aware of what you're eating.

Still Not Full? That's Emotional Eating

You ate a box of donuts? But you're still hungry? That's emotional hunger. Your stomach is almost like a bottomless pit. You keep eating more and more. Often until it's too late and you are uncomfortably stuffed. In contrast, when you feel satisfied because your stomach is 80% full, this is physical hunger.

Negative Emotions are Linked to Emotional Hunger:

Guilt, shame, regret are all emotions linked to emotional hunger. If you feel bad after you eat, it's most likely because you know that you're not eating for nutritional reasons and you ate to help yourself feel better emotionally.

Emotional hunger vs. Physical hunger

Emotional hunger comes on suddenly

Physical hunger comes on gradually

Emotional hunger feels like it needs to be satisfied instantly

Physical hunger can wait

Emotional hunger craves specific comfort foods

Physical hunger is open to options—lots of things sound good

Emotional hunger isn't satisfied with a full stomach.

Physical hunger stops when you're full

Emotional eating triggers feelings of guilt, powerlessness, and shame

Eating to satisfy physical hunger doesn't make you feel bad about yourself

Thou Shalt Not Be Triggered

VIPs, it is your responsibility to put a stop to all triggers that are setting off a crazy downward spiral of emotional eating. But how do you know when you're being triggered? This is your fun work to do. You must identify your own personal triggers. And then remove them. What people, situations, activities, or feelings make you snatch out for the instant comfort of a big bowl of fettuccine alfredo? Let's get real here. Most emotional eating is associated to bad feelings, so who makes you feel bad? Who disturbs your inner peace? What thoughts from your past force you into an emotional eating binge? We must stop all of this right here right now. Replace them with positive triggers! It's that simple!

LIST OF NEGATIVE TRIGGERS:

Stuffing emotions – Eating can be a way to temporarily silence or "stuff down" uncomfortable emotions, including anger, fear, sadness, anxiety, loneliness, resentment, and shame. While you're numbing yourself with food, you can avoid the difficult emotions you'd rather not feel.

Dear Stress, I Hate You! – Stress makes you hungry. It's that simple. It's not just in your mind. living under a constant stream of stress in our crazy lives, our bodies naturally produce high levels of the stress hormone cortisol. This ugly hormone makes you crave for crunchy, fried, salty, and sugary foods. These foods give you instant satisfaction and a pop of energy. So what's the solution? Control the stress in your life. Because the more uncontrolled stress you experience every day, the more likely you are to turn to food for an emotional fix.

Having an Empty Calendar is Like Dating the Devil. Being Bored is Bad!

To cut through the chase, when you're bored that can lead to mindless eating or just eating out of boredom. Whenever you feel alone, or bored, or isolated, you ever simply find yourself eating just to fill that void in your life? When you feel bored, eating is a common go-to activity that will occupy your mouth and also fill up your time. Not good! What's the solution? Keep your calendar full of positive activities that make you feel purposeful and satisfied. A lot of times we eat because we feel our lives are not purpose-driven and weren't dissatisfied with ourselves.

Food is Linked to Happy Memories

Think about it, when you were a child, and it was your birthday, people put you in the center of the room, put a hat on top of your head, sing to you, buy you presents, light sparklers on a big mountain of frosted covered sugar. So, as soon as you take a bite of the cake with a side of ice cream, you associate that with love, comfort, happiness, joy, and feeling at ease and celebrated. No wonder we are addicted to sugar! We must break those old childhood memories that associate eating bad food with comfort and love.

What about our weekly "pizza parties" with your friends? Everyone's waiting for the pizza man to deliver the pepperoni heavenly pie! Everybody was happy, and in a good mood. Everyone ate together and had a great time. No wonder we always want to grab a slice of a deep dish as we have linked it to cam, festivities, and being happy with our friends. And yes, these unhealthy food associations and habits can often carry over into adulthood.

Mom's homemade apple pie? Our eating may be driven by nostalgia such as baking and eating cookies with your grandma. Just from our childhood, we've been set up for failure when it comes to eating healthy. We must change these associations and I'm here to help you! A VIP woman always links pleasure to eating lean, clean and green, and associates pain to eating empty calories that are laden with sugar and fat.

"Feed Your Feelings" in Healthy Ways

You must get conscious control over your eating habits in order for your new land clean and green food plan to work. We must know how to manage our emotions in a way that doesn't involve eating bad food. Because diets always fail because they offer logical nutritional advice, which only works if you have gained authority over your eating habits. So don't eat with your emotions!

Let's finally take off the emotional eating vines that have held us hostage for so long. In the next section I'm going to offer solid ways to help you stop eating emotionally so you can fulfill yourself emotionally in other ways besides food.

If you're depressed or lonely, log into the VIP chat room or our "Faith-Book" Page", or call someone who always makes you feel better, play with your pets!

If you're anxious, burn your nervous energy by enjoying a JNL VIP workout, a Zen in 10 Meditation, or a guided meditation on our e-library at JNLVIP.com

If you're exhausted, treat yourself with a power nap, a hot cup of tea, take a bath, light some scented candles, or wrap yourself in a warm blanket.

If you're bored, check in with your fellow VIP sisters online! We are always here for you! Or watch a comedy video, get outside or find a hobby that makes you happy!

As you can see, a VIP woman has crushed her old archaic wiring of emotional eating! We can now finally say goodbye to emotional eating, and hello to eating hot tamale for a VIP lifestyle!

EAT TO LIVE, DONT LIVE TO EAT!

VIPs in this section, you will find a super useful grocery list of some of my very own JNL-Approved staple foods that you should stock up on during your weekly grocery hauls!

Feel free to bring this list to your farmers market or grocery store with you!

PRODUCE

All vegetables.

All fruits

Aim for Organic if possible

HEALTHY FATS

Olive oil

Coconut Oil

Unsalted Nuts

Unsalted Seeds

Avocado

Sesame Oil

Ghee, Clarified Butter

LEAN SOURCES OF PROTEIN

Eggs

Fish

Poultry

Lean red meat (in moderation)

WHAT TO AVOID

Fried foods

Foods high in preservatives

Fast food

Sweets/Sugar

Simple Carbs

Butter

Any refined oils

Margarine

Corn Oil

Soybean Oil

In Closing, Remember Who You Are! You are a VIP Woman!

A VIP woman knows her worth and goes for what she wants! She is unapologetically herself. She does what makes her happy. She's resilient. She's flexible. She never breaks. She plows right through any roadblock. She has a warrior spirit. She lives a passionate life, full of zest, vigor, fierce focus, and with relentless energy to slay her goals!

Thank you for taking the time to invest in yourself by reading this book! May everything you learned bless you tenfold beyond your wildest dreams! And remember, I'm just an email, WhatsApp, GM, text message away! Please share your success stories with me! Because your success is my success!

In love and light,

Coach Jennifer Nicole Lee

www.JenniferNicoleLee

www.JNLVIP.com

www.JNLCoaching.com

Social Media:

www.JNLYoutube.com

www.JenniferNicoleLee.com

www.JNLVIP.com

@JenniferNicoleLee

Made in USA - Kendallville, IN
1213896_9781952903076
12.15.2020 1317